Mike Burnette is a great friend and leader who inspires me with his gift of stepping outside of the collective comfort zone. He will do whatever it takes to encounter the heart of Jesus and reflect his compassion to humanity. That's why *Parable Church* is a must-read! If you're looking for a fresh perspective to strip away the clutter and to learn the culture of God's kingdom in fresh ways, this book is it.

>   **PASTOR DINO RIZZO**, executive director,
>   ARC (Association of Related Churches)

Pastor Mike distills foundational principles on the purpose, methods, and value of the church as the means of growing God's kingdom in only the way a pastor of one of the fastest-growing churches in America could. His words are detailed enough for the wisest scholar, yet simple enough for a beginner to enjoy. Church leaders need to read this book and then lead their flock to become a parable church.

>   **DR. MARK GREEN**, US congressman
>   and former special operator, US Army

My dear friend Mike Burnette is an inspiring and gifted communicator. In this powerful book, he unpacks the parables of Jesus to help us understand the difference between *doing* church and actually *being* Christ's church. Pastor Mike exposes the spirit of "religious people rules" and reveals the true culture of the kingdom of God and the heart of the Father.

>   **NANCY ALCORN**, founder and
>   president of Mercy Multiplied

In a time when many people are being forced to rethink church, *Parable Church* brings a fresh opportunity to reimagine the way Jesus wants his church to gather.

>   **GABE LYONS**, president of Q Ideas
>   and author of *Good Faith*

I've often said that if Jesus walked the earth today, he'd be a filmmaker. The best filmmakers are the storytellers, and Jesus told stories. When his adversaries asked "gotcha" questions, Jesus always had an answer in the form of a story. In parables. I honor my friend Mike Burnette for unpacking the truth within these amazing stories for all generations. This book is a must-read!

> **ISRAEL HOUGHTON,** Grammy Award–winning
> songwriter and worship leader

This book is one of the most significant books I've read as a church leader. My friend Mike Burnette has masterfully revealed the intent of Jesus' parables and how to live them out in the life of the local church. It's only when we transcend the religiosity of *doing* and embrace the relationship of *being* that we will truly manifest God's will here on earth. *Parable Church* is a must-read for anyone who is serious about aligning with the mission and message of Jesus Christ.

> **DR. JOSEPH W. WALKER, III,** Mount
> Zion Baptist Church, presiding bishop of
> Full Gospel Baptist Church Fellowship

In *Parable Church*, Mike Burnette doesn't give generic leadership platitudes as a substitute way to build a church; instead, he insightfully pulls leadership gems from the soil of Jesus' use of parables—stories that were valuable not only to the original listening audience but also to those of us eager to build churches that reflect God's kingdom. You'll enjoy the treasures he excavates. Act quickly to embed them in the soil of your leadership.

> **WAYNE FRANCIS,** lead pastor of
> The Life Church, New York, and
> coauthor of *Black Fist, White Knuckles*

Stinking brilliant! Out of a hundred books on how to create healthy church culture, this is the one that stands out. Mike Burnette gives a ridiculously simple filter through which to rethink church—*the parables of Jesus*. Mike finds a way to bypass all of the silly church debates in the most lifegiving way, and then he shares the values through which vision can thrive. This book is the ultimate skeleton key to unlock the door and bring resolution to almost any church dispute.

PETER HAAS, pastor of Substance Church and performer, DJ, and producer for SubstanceVariant.com

Before I read a book, I ask two basic questions: Does the author have credibility? And do they have something meaningful to say? Mike Burnette scores on both counts. *Parable Church* offers a fresh approach to a timely topic. This book will inspire you to see your place in the world differently. On a scale of 1 to 10, this book is a 10.

HAL DONALDSON, CEO, Convoy of Hope

The church is the primary instrument that God uses to expand his kingdom here on earth. Being the church and leading in the church are sacred and privileged opportunities. My friend Mike Burnette has brilliantly combined his life experiences and the parables of Jesus to help the reader do both. His insights on Jesus' parables will deepen your faith and strengthen your leadership. Enjoy your journey through *Parable Church*.

DOUG CLAY, general superintendent of the Assemblies of God

Mike Burnette is an emerging leader on whom God's hand obviously rests. He has been given rich insights into dynamic keys for Christian living. Mike unpacks the parables of Jesus in a fresh way, offering pragmatic thoughts based on biblical truths and translating them into everyday life and leadership. *Parable Church* is a must-read!

GERALD BROOKS, pastor of Grace Outreach Center, Gerald Brooks Ministries

Mike Burnette helps all of us as leaders understand the power of building a church on the foundation of "being the church" and not just doing church. This is a deep dive into the countercultural building of God's kingdom through the power of parables and storytelling.

BRAD LOMENICK, founder, BLINC, and author of *H3 Leadership* and *The Catalyst Leader*

PARABLE
CHURCH

*How the Teachings of Jesus Shape
the Culture of Our Faith*

MIKE BURNETTE
WITH JOHN DRIVER

**ZONDERVAN
REFLECTIVE**

ZONDERVAN REFLECTIVE

Parable Church
Copyright © 2021 by Mike Burnette

Requests for information should be addressed to:
Zondervan, *3900 Sparks Dr. SE, Grand Rapids, Michigan 49546*

Zondervan titles may be purchased in bulk for educational, business, fundraising, or sales promotional use. For information, please email SpecialMarkets@Zondervan.com.

ISBN 978-0-310-11301-0 (softcover)

ISBN 978-0-310-11303-4 (audio)

ISBN 978-0-310-11302-7 (ebook)

Published in association with the literary agency of Wolgemuth & Associates, Inc.

Cover design: Thinkpen Design
Cover photo: © Lana Veshta / Shutterstock
Interior design: Kait Lamphere

Printed in the United States of America

21 22 23 24 25 26 27 28 29 30 /LSC/ 15 14 13 12 11 10 9 8 7 6 5 4 3 2 1

To my best friend, Stephanie—
thanks for believing in me
and for your consistent encouragement!

And to the amazing people of LifePoint Church—
you have given me the greatest privilege
to serve as your pastor
and to see this book play out in real time.
Philippians 1:27!

CONTENTS

PART 3: The Parable of the Talents

FOREWORD

I have always been in church. *Always.*

Since the day I was born, church was like my second home. I grew up in a formal denominational church, and I assumed most churches were like my own—mostly boring but somehow important. The liturgy didn't do much for me, but I enjoyed being part of a community filled with my family and friends. I didn't love it, but I didn't hate it either. Church was just a part of my family's tradition and, therefore, part of my life.

But my assumptions changed one Sunday evening when I visited my friend's church. Almost immediately, I realized the people in the pews around me loved God in ways I had never experienced. They made the Christian faith look so attractive. For them, living for Jesus was like breathing: effortless and essential at the same time. They had something—joy, peace, confidence, purpose—that I lacked but desperately wanted to experience.

The pastor's message that night pierced my heart in a way no other preaching had touched me. At some point during that service, I realized I didn't love God like these people loved him because I didn't *know* God the way they knew him. I had been trying to earn my way to heaven, doing whatever it took to please an inscrutable, grumpy old God.

One good thing about growing up in church: I understood the Bible well enough to recognize it was the only authority I could trust for the ultimate truth of how to know God. So I started nervously turning those thin, tissue-like pages until I began to see words and phrases pop off the page at me. I had one of those classic red-letter editions of the Bible with the words of Christ printed in bright crimson. Surely, that red ink had been used for such a moment as this!

I was only a few pages into Matthew when a passage jumped off the page: "Not everyone who says to me, 'Lord, Lord,' will enter the kingdom of heaven, but the one who does the will of my Father who is in heaven. On that day many will say to me, 'Lord, Lord, did we not prophesy in your name, and cast out demons in your name, and do many mighty works in your name?' And then will I declare to them, 'I never knew you'" (Matthew 7:21–23).

Jesus' words sent chills down my spine.

They described me perfectly because I had spent my whole life calling him Lord for no other reason than because it was what everyone had told me to do. I had confessed with my mouth that I wanted to be saved, but I had never surrendered my heart. I had invited God into my life, but I had left the door locked from the inside.

That night I realized the truth for the first time. God wasn't looking for my religious actions or which church I attended. He never wanted me to do things for him to earn his love and forgiveness and grace. He wasn't grumpy or hard to please—*he wanted to know me!*

Tears welled in my eyes, and my heart drummed so fast I thought it might burst through my chest. I got on my knees and planted my elbows into my bed as I clasped my hands to pray. "If you'll give me another chance, Lord, I'll love you," I said. "I want to know you. Really know you."

I felt the presence of the Spirit within me. In that moment, God became more than the God I had read about or the Creator of the universe. He became my Friend, my Savior, my heavenly Father, my Daddy.

Almost four decades of ministry later, I still believe this is what people want.

They want to *know* God.

Visiting my friend's church rocked my understanding of what church could be and rolled away my false assumptions about who God is. That experience ignited a longing to know God the same way they did, to serve him with everything I have in order for others to know him that way, and to help people relate to God as part of a family of believers.

Over the years, God's Word and my ministry experience have shown me many different ways to do church. But churches that reflect God's love with the greatest impact tend to have some key elements in common—qualities that my friend Mike Burnette sees clearly in the parables Jesus told his followers.

In the pages that follow, Mike helps us see these dynamic church qualities by exploring how parables teach us heavenly concepts grounded in earthly situations. Simple but never simplistic, timeless and timely, accessible and relatable, Jesus' stories show us how God is like a patient, loving Father running to hug his wayward children when they finally come home. How seeds must be planted in the right kind of soil to grow and produce fruit. How taking risks with the resources we're given is essential to please the One who gave us those resources. Simply put, parables provide illustrated instructions for knowing how to relate to God and other people—a fundamental goal of every Bible-based, God-honoring, Christ-following church.

Mike knows that the parables of Jesus have so much to teach us—both as his followers and as pastors and leaders of his church.

If you long to lead a community of believers whose contagious love will be noticed by every visitor to your church, this book is for you. If you want a deeper, closer relationship with the Lord, Mike's insightful wisdom on Jesus' parables will open your eyes. Whether you're answering God's call to serve or seeking fellowship with a faith-filled family of believers, *Parable Church* will forever change the way you view the body of Christ—and your role in it!

Chris Hodges, pastor,
Church of the Highlands

CHAPTER 1

JESUS SAID WHAT?

Jesus never told us how to "do church."

Believe me, I often wish he would have. That would have made my life—and probably yours too—so much easier. But he didn't.[1]

Just so we can get acquainted, I'm a pastor of a growing church, but that is not at all what I set out to do. I didn't *really* grow up in church, if you know what I mean. I became a follower of Jesus on Halloween in my senior year of high school. I attended one church in high school and another in college, and then I became a staff member at the second church.

At the time, I was 6 feet, 6 inches tall and 260 pounds. You might guess that I spent most of my time on the football field or basketball court. You would be mistaken. I never was a *linebacker*; instead I stood on the *back line* of the choir. I went to the University of Tennessee on a full music scholarship and had every intention of becoming a professional opera singer. Yes, you read that right.

I had no interest in pursuing a career in ministry, but my pastor saw something in this misfit that I definitely couldn't see in myself, and he invited me to join his staff, promising to teach me how to "do church." It was an unassuming and auspicious start, to say the least, and I had a very steep learning curve.

1

I went from performing Puccini to preaching Paul's epistles —not exactly an easy transition or the start to the world's most impressive bio. But today I've been in full-time ministry for more than two decades, and I now feel more comfortable reading Dietrich Bonhoeffer than singing Johannes Brahms's *Lieder*. (Pardon my nerdy musical references. I can tell you're excited for what lies ahead.)

It is now probably evident that when I started in ministry, I didn't know anything at all about "doing church." And I'm not the only one. From guys like me to biblical scholars, many of us feel this way. The topic of how to do church is important, but it's crazy that most of our conversations in and about the modern church are consumed by things that Jesus never directly addressed.

- Is the pastor a solid communicator who can be both funny and profound, with a hint of edginess?
- Is the worship team talented and able to choose relevant songs that people will like?
- Is there a vibrant children's ministry that will keep kids excited, engaged, and out of their parents' hair for at least an hour? Which reminds me, should a service ever be shorter than an hour?
- And should the pastor wear a three-piece suit, or should he rock skinny jeans?

Some of these may seem more trivial than others. I don't intend to downplay—or even address—issues like these in this book. Jesus had much to say about the church, but when we dive a little deeper, we will find that these statements were mostly unrelated to stylistic issues or contextual trends. He didn't say much of anything about many of the topics that fill our blogs and libraries today. He didn't address church leadership hierarchies,

local governmental and constitutional structures, elder development and placement, the pros and cons of denominational fellow-
ships, deacon committees, long-term organizational guidelines
for distributing food and resources to the poor and hungry, what
level of seminary education is necessary (or at least wise) for pastoral qualification, what version of the Bible should be used, or
whether it's okay to use saltine crackers instead of real loaves of
unleavened bread for Communion.

Jesus' disciples and the early church leaders who served with
and after them addressed some of these issues, but Jesus himself
did not. Honestly, much of their writing on the subject was contextual and descriptive, not necessarily prescriptive. We debate these
distinctions to this day. But Jesus? He did not debate them at all.

Obviously, he said a lot though. He dealt with his people's
hearts—with the culture of his kingdom he wanted beating
within those hearts. He spoke about grace, generosity, inclusiv-
ity, mercy, salvation. And he spoke a lot about what it means to
belong to his kingdom. He emphatically said he would build his
church; he just didn't say much about how those of us who labor
with him are supposed to do it—at least not in the ways we might
hope for or expect.

If we juxtapose Jesus' silence on this topic with the fact that
we are constantly asking questions and seeking advice on how to
do church, what can we conclude? Perhaps that we inadvertently
separate the ways we do church from the words of Jesus because
we have so much to do and worry about that Jesus never directly
addressed in the Gospels.

I invite you to approach the idea of church differently, not
just in the ways we "do church"—how we accomplish our weekly
practices and services—but in a way that is much simpler and
more applicable, unique, and kingdom accomplishable. You see,
Jesus may not have told us how to *do* church, but through his

teachings—and, more specifically, his parables—he shows us how to *be* his church. He reveals how his church can and should reflect the culture of the kingdom of heaven.

Every kingdom has its own culture: England, Zulu, Apple, Microsoft, and even your grandma's house. Each of these "kingdoms" has a unique environment, language, vibe, DNA, value system, and the like. Being in these places means experiencing these cultures. Likewise, the kingdom of heaven has a culture, and this culture is what Jesus continues to unveil through his parables. They show us what the kingdom of heaven feels like—and thus what the culture of our churches should feel like.

And when I use the phrase "feel like" in relation to this culture, I'm not talking about the smells or colors of the rooms, the touchy-feely emotions, or even the attempts to create certain atmospheres with smoke and lighting designed for those who attend our services. This is not *that* kind of feeling. After all, rightly being God's church won't always "feel" easy or comfortable. It can be downright hard.

I am referring to the general vibe that someone experiences when they come into contact with the Lord's church, a sense of heavenly encounter that people should gain when they are around Jesus' people, mainly because Jesus' people have actually been hanging out with Jesus and emulating him.

This brings us back to Jesus' words, or the lack thereof. Above all other techniques, Jesus chose parables as his communication method of choice. It was almost as if he knew we would be prone to create stringent, boxy, legalistic checklists out of whatever he said, regardless of what he meant. If Jesus told us to sing two hymns at every church service (which is a fine thing to do if you like to), we would tar and feather anyone who dared to sing one hymn or three hymns. We would spend our time policing the number of songs instead of actually singing them with passion and purpose.

In all my years of studying, visiting people, or providing leadership in church, I've seen many traditions that are upheld and lauded. In the liturgical or high church setting, there are sacred moments or elements, like the tradition of carrying out the preaching Bible, escorting the pastor to the pulpit, and bowing down to the remaining elements of the Eucharist after Mass. In some evangelical or Pentecostal circles, we see a focus on "feeling God move"—keeping up with how many times someone falls backward or speaks in tongues in a worship service—or whether the preacher "really preached," which gauges how emotional, boisterous, or loud he was and whether he portrayed a certain sense of honor that resulted in the maintaining of distance from pastors or leaders. Without commentary on any of these ecclesiastical choices, none of them are actually discussed by Jesus as a part of "building his church," and yet they have become focal points for the way we have come to "do church."

We tend to lean toward the technicalities of church rather than the disposition of the One who breathed it into existence. In other words, we tend to *legalize*. Through the parables, Jesus chose instead to *conceptualize*, to throw us off the scent of our endless checklists while still leaving us completely immersed in the aroma of his kingdom.

The parables are abstract enough to keep us from making them into laws but clear enough to help us understand what matters to God. Jesus talked about lost things. He talked about hurting people. He talked about the condition of people's hearts. He talked about the gifts and expectations of divine stewardship. He talked about radical forgiveness that resulted in parties for those who dare to come home to the open arms of the Father who is always watching the horizon, willing to sprint toward any once-was-lost child.

I invite you to be God's church in a way that reflects these and many other cultural values of Christ's kingdom, the things that matter to God. Because one of the most significant things about being God's church is that everything important to him becomes important to us as well.

Also, if you are reading through these pages with me, then you probably fall into one of two categories: a church leader or staff member, or a Christian who attends church and desires to see her become all that God intends her to be. Whichever you are, please know that I'm writing this for you—both of you. I am a pastor and will often talk to pastors, mainly because many of my stories come out of that context. However, I'm also writing this to the people whom I pastor—and to you.

Sometimes I will be writing specifically to leaders, and sometimes I will be writing to everyone (and I'll usually tell you when I switch between the two). However, these stories and principles are usually not leader- or member-specific—that is to say, they are for all of us, regardless of our role in God's church. And we all have a role, as we will soon discover. Even if it seems I'm only speaking to pastors in some sections, it will be extremely helpful for everyone to pay attention to what Jesus is teaching us through his parables. A huge problem in the church today is the dichotomy that exists between leaders and members, as if their missions are somehow different. Yes, some may "do church" as a career, but "being the church" is the privilege and responsibility of every believer—which is why Jesus was speaking to all of us through the parables, as does this book.

Jesus used stories that were effectively illustrative—some perhaps made up on the spot and others reflecting events that actually happened—in order to prove his points. If you will indulge me, let me begin to prove my point by telling you the first of a few true stories.

THE REAL JESUS

Where you do life reveals a lot about what you do with that life.

I do life in one of the fastest growing cities you've probably never heard of: Clarksville, Tennessee. Of course, you may know of it if you happen to be a closet fan of the old 1960s band The Monkees and their hit "Last Train to Clarksville." I am not a huge fan of the song, but I am a huge fan of our city—and especially of the people who live here. Among other things, Clarksville is a military town, nestled on the banks of the Cumberland River just across the Kentucky line and the Fort Campbell army post, where the famed 101st Airborne is located. As you might imagine, many soldiers and their families find their way to our church.

That's how I first met Blane.

Blane was not your average soldier. He was a decorated combat medic who had been trained and considered for many unique missions. (Who knows how many death-defying experiences he actually participated in while on active duty?) Blane was a hero in every sense of the word.

This elite level of training and toughness also made Blane a little, well, tough. He was covered in tattoos—full sleeves on both arms. His concept of "church people" like me wasn't exactly positive. He had grown up in an environment that taught him to expect a nun's high-velocity ruler to crack down on his knuckles when he got out of line.[2] What should have fed and softened his heart had starved and hardened it instead.

It's not surprising that Blane became highly competitive, always attempting to outdo everyone around him in everything imaginable. He wanted to drink more. Fight more. Get more girls' numbers. Blane became a master sergeant of one-upmanship.

Then one day, one of his military buddies he was always trying to one-up became a Christ follower, and Blane encountered the first thing in life in which he had no desire to outdo the next guy. No, he wanted to stay far away from what he considered a ridiculous religious game his friend was now playing.

Even so, Blane's comrade was relentless, constantly inviting him to experience what was happening to the people who gathered at his church. But Blane repeatedly insisted he was having none of it. He had a lot of his own commentary about church, specifically that churches were full of hypocrites who would judge him for his tattoos and lifestyle, only wanted his money, wanted to convert his politics to the "right" side, and didn't like sinners. He was no idiot; their only goal was to convert him, and he could see right through their ruse.

This went on for some time. Blane dug his heels in the ground, but his friend was insistent: "Man, this church just *feels* different. They love people like you and me. This is not what you expect."

The day finally came when Blane caved and showed up—by himself. He got out of his car and immediately rolled his sleeves all the way down to his wrists to cover his tattoos, buttoning his sleeves for good measure. As he walked across the parking lot, he began to sweat (and not because of the heat). He waited for someone to mouth off to him about his appearance. To this day, I'm grateful no one did; Blane was an avid fighter, and sometimes he would go to bars and pick fights just to stay sharp with his combat skills. This callous warrior—someone many churches would never expect to show up—approached the front door of the one place in the world he had sworn he would never go.

But standing in the lobby was a man named Larry who actually was expecting him—or at least someone like him. Larry, who goes by "Pop," is a retired Navy command master chief. He is no stranger to military toughness, but his heart was divinely softened and rewired many years ago to love and connect with people in a unique way. Pop was greeting people as they walked into the lobby that day, so he was the first person Blane met—and let me tell you, Pop was *not* who Blane expected to meet.

"Hello, young man! My name's Pop. What's yours?"

"I'm Blane," he mumbled suspiciously.

Pop reached out to shake his hand but then unexpectedly pulled him in for a hug. They were two battle-tested warriors who had just met, hugging each other in the lobby of a church. Nothing to see here.

"I'm so glad you're here, Blane!"

His sleeves were still buttoned down tight, but something deep inside Blane was beginning to loosen.

I was starting a new message series that day about Christians and the church. No doubt, Blane expected me to defend all the things he hated about church, but that's not exactly what happened. Instead, quoting several books and other research on the subject, I admitted that the church in America seems to have lost its prophetic edge.[3] We've decimated our witness and influence with the world outside our walls because we've become more well known for hypocrisy and judgmentalism inside our walls. Here's how many people perceive the church: we're all Republicans; we hate homosexuals; and we only really care about money and conversions, not actual people. In my message, I concluded that the world doesn't want anything to do with this kind of church anymore, and it is right to feel that way.

Blane, who was now sitting with his friend, leaned toward him and said, "These are the same reasons I told you I don't want to go to this or any church! And now your pastor is agreeing with me?" If something had loosened earlier, now it was beginning to break. God was doing something in Blane. Over the following weeks, we endeavored to reveal the real culture of Jesus' kingdom, thereby showing him a different Jesus from the only versions he had ever seen. We showed him the real Jesus.

Blane is not alone in mistaking the identity of Jesus because of a random run-in with one or more of his people. Many church leaders fail to realize the church is expected—by the Bible and the culture that couldn't care less about the Bible—to be an accurate reflection of the real Jesus, not just his commandments or moral viewpoints but also, and first, his personal temperament and the way he approached people. For better or worse, people predominantly make their decisions about the kind of guy Jesus is when they cross paths with his people.

We shouldn't be surprised by this. Jesus said it would happen.[4]

Try this mental exercise. Clear your mind of whatever impressions you have of Jesus. Imagine that you met Jesus in person for the first time, and the relationship goes deep very quickly. You have meals together; you travel together; you listen to him speak and watch him engage people in real time. You observe his prayer times; you hold his personal effects while he lays hands on a woman who needs healing; and you sit together with him around the campfire at night. What would this level of engagement with the actual Jesus reveal to you about the identity, nature, and character of Jesus? What is he like? How does he talk about and treat people? What stirs him and who becomes a welcomed interruption to Jesus? What does he care about?

Does the Jesus you're imagining excite you? Does this Jesus seem authentic and attractive to you? Is he worth following to the ends of the earth?

Now, ask yourself this question in juxtaposition: Does *that* Jesus seem familiar to you based on your interaction with his followers? Does Jesus resemble the church people with whom you've interacted? Finally, try reflecting on this scenario from the perspective of a first-time guest at a church full of Jesus' followers. To be clear, this exercise is important for both church leaders and church members, though each of you may have to suspend something in order to honestly engage it—after all, whether we are vocational pastors or simply disciples, we are all producing these impressions . . . and we should all be highly aware of what those who don't know Jesus are learning about him from his followers.

Here's the thing: this is not an imaginary scenario. It's happening every day to millions of people. The problem is not that who we are as the church leaves people with impressions and conclusions about Jesus himself; that's supposed to happen. The problem is that those impressions and conclusions are flawed, and we often do not accurately reflect and imitate Jesus' temperament and disposition toward people. Perhaps it's because we ourselves are also a little confused about the real personality of the real Jesus. We seem to grasp the basics of his theology, but we're not sure about his attitude or ethics toward us, so our attitude toward others follows suit. Of course, we could never admit this because, after all, we are "church people" who are supposed to know better.

By the way, this is not a slam on church people, but rather a realization that we sometimes allow our idealized or flawed perceptions of Jesus (or self-imposed expectations of life as a follower) to overshadow the real Jesus. I'm encouraged that he can and does still work through us in spite of our issues, because he loves to shine brightly through broken people. In your brokenness, this is a call to better reflect the ethic of Jesus as the world watches what he is doing in us to faithfully and graciously heal us—and not only us, but also those with whom we interact.

Theological statements, doctrinal declarations, and cutesy acrostics of our core values all have their place and should not be excluded (well, except perhaps the acrostics). The answer for the church is not to become such a "super-seeker" environment that sacred beliefs and practices are barely even mentioned, but neither is it to be more defined by these statements and structures than we are mobilized to live them out in honest, authentic relationships that reflect the nature and personality of Jesus himself. Surely such a Christ-centered belief and community should be the daily stuff of actually being and making disciples, right? We'll get to that.

For now you may be wondering, what about Blane? And what about all the other people out there who seem to have trouble meeting the real Jesus because they've only heard the wrong kinds of stories about him? It just so happens that Jesus' own stories are a huge part of his strategy to communicate to people—believers and unbelievers alike—more than just theological facts or moralistic guidelines. His stories clear up so much of the confusion about who he is, what he's about, and what matters to him, especially if we read them with fresh eyes.

WHAT PARABLES REVEAL

My heart for Blane was that he would gain an understanding of the heart of the real Jesus that is vividly revealed in the stories Jesus famously told. These stories are also known as parables. Parables—and he told quite a few of them—were Jesus' preferred method for creating word pictures to colorfully portray the way he *feels* about people, including people like Blane who thought Jesus and his people just wanted to roll up their sleeves and start judging or fixing him.

After our church experienced multiple years of rapid growth, pastors began calling me to ask for help or coaching so they could somehow secure the same results we had experienced. I often was asked about our "secret," or some form of "What three or four things did you do to experience such fast growth?" The truth is, we have no secrets, and I couldn't imagine packaging a growth plan into three or four quick tips.

So I began to pray and really search the Scriptures for God's plan for growth, what the Bible suggests about healthy growth, and what I could share with pastors that would help them. I kept coming back to the idea that culture is king, and like my pastor, Chris Hodges, says, "Culture always trumps vision." So Jesus said he would build his church but didn't tell us how. Then he taught these parables, which revealed his preferred culture, so I studied his parables . . . a lot![5]

When I did my study of all of the parables Jesus taught and what they revealed, I was so excited that they motivated me to pursue the concept of this book. By studying the parables of Jesus, I discovered a culture that Jesus was trying to reveal—the culture of another kingdom. Throughout his parables, Jesus taught us how he will always make room for others, search for the missing, make a way for grace to abound, and more. The culture revealed throughout the parables is so different from anything our world had ever known—and often, it is also different from what the world knows of his church today.

Imagine Blane's surprise when he began to learn that the culture Jesus reveals in his stories is something completely different from what he had experienced or expected. Among many other things, it is generous, not stingy. Celebratory, not drab. Merciful, not judgmental. Selfless, not demanding. Encouraging, not harsh. Honest, not deceptive. Patient, not easily deterred. Diverse, not monochromatic. Caring, not cruel. Scripturally sound, not man-made. Restorative, not destructive. Creative, not boring. Grateful, not entitled. Hopeful, not heavy. Grace-filled, not works-based or works-demanding. Inviting, not standoffish. Always open to second chances—to endless chances, in fact—provided by an boundless grace paid at an infinite cost.

A study of all thirty-seven parables reveals a culture that is extremely warm and inviting, to the point that every one of Jesus' parables includes an invitation to this kind of environment and never to one that is negative, repulsive, condemning, or exclusive of those who need grace.

A few weeks after Blane's first visit, we threw a major party for him as he was baptized. Why? Because we know that Jesus cares deeply about throwing parties for those he loves who come home. Years later, Blane is still with us—still helping people just like him get past their faulty expectations of the culture of Christ's kingdom. We didn't "save" Blane. We were, however, used by God to express to him some of the things God cares about most deeply. We helped turn over the soil of his heart so that when the seed of the real message of Christ was planted therein—the one where Jesus loves you enough to rescue you with the priceless ransom of his own life long before you had the chance to ask for it or try unsuccessfully to earn it—it had a better chance to take root and grow. Blane is a great reminder of just how amazing God's kingdom really is. It is full of love, grace, forgiveness, generosity, patience, broken people, and a perfect God.

Unfortunately, what Blane expected the message of Christ to be is exactly what many people experience every Sunday in churches filled with well-meaning people. They are working for a kingdom—just not the one Jesus talks about in his parables. Too many suspicions like Blane's are confirmed by those who should be displaying the immeasurable beauty of grace radiating through transparent brokenness together. Their approach is not at all what God desires for us, so it's no wonder so many people are confused about his intentions, leaving no room in their lives for him or his people.

This is not just about tattoos, bar fights, or lifestyles; this is about the presence or absence of a deeply embedded under-standing concerning everything God desires most for all people and how these desires are supposed to be most fully realized and expressed through his church—often the very people who instead mask it with hypocrisy, judgmentalism, self-assured layers of righteousness or "right-ness," and cultural disconnectedness.

If *where* you do life reveals a lot about *what* you do with that life, it's time to acknowledge that the church is supposed to be a different kind of "where" than it often is. It may not be the last train to Clarksville, but God's most amazing intention for all people has tragically become one of the last places they would ever want to be. Many of us have read headlines about fallen pastors or heard horror stories about strange behaviors or beliefs within churches. They may seem isolated or not *that* big of a deal. But these behaviors and practices shape the experiences and the culture of those who visit and belong and may well have contributed to the overall decline in church life today. But there is good news: I believe the parables are a great opportunity to return to the foundations—to an understanding not just of what Jesus tells us to do or not do, but also of what he cares about the most.

LOOKING FOR LIFE IN NEW PLACES

As we sit together in these pages, I hope you will allow me to either reveal to you some new perspectives from Jesus' parables or remind you of some things you already know but haven't necessarily made priorities in your thoughts, decisions, or leadership. This process must begin with the way you think, that is, with the most cluttered place within you—your mind. We're all a product of the environment and the experiences of our childhood, for better or for worse. These things affect our mindsets, our expectations, and our reactions in ways we do not necessarily realize.

For my friend Blane, the judgment and rejection he had received from "church people" over the years galvanized his belief that God couldn't be trusted, much less his people. He buttoned down his sleeves to cover what he was convinced would be the first of many deal breakers, but someone—well, several "someones" in this case—lived out a different culture in front of him by caring for the things Jesus cares about. And then Jesus did something through that tiny hole in his armor that no one else could ever do.

Blane's friend who attended our church cared enough to keep chipping away at Blane's resistance, choosing not to take serious offense at the many offensive things he was saying about Christians—about him. Pop cared by being ready to embrace him—literally—even though it's uncommon for military men to do such things with strangers. My part was the easiest. I cared enough not to patronize him with false claims about the state of the church in today's culture. Instead, I tried to meet him right where he was. The culture of Christ's kingdom teaches us to not fear real conversations with people about Jesus on their own terms.

For all of us in Blane's story, there was no agenda except to be open to caring about what Jesus cares about so he could do something in Blane that none of us could do in a thousand years of well-wishing or whitewashing with religious nonsense over his poor choices and bad attitudes.

In the same way, I have no agenda with our time together in these pages except to do the same. If you're reading this, it is already a huge step because it means you are opening your mind to new ideas, even if only begrudgingly because a friend asked you to do so. Regardless, I am truly honored, and I want you to know I have no delusions of grandeur about my words. I am not anything special—and anyone who knows me can verify this claim.

I am, however, experiencing something special each and every day with the friends I run with in our church. It is something that none of us could produce on our own; it is truly greater than the sum of our broken parts. I am a part of something I previously could have only dreamed of.

And the thing is, God wants you to be part of it too, even if you don't live in my town. God wants you to experience a life with other broken-being-rescued people that is authentic, fun, fulfilling, transformative, and eternal. I know, I know—this sounds a lot like rhetoric and may sound nothing like the life of the church people you've known up to now (perhaps even including yourself). I couldn't be more adamant that it doesn't have to be that way. There are people who are learning to experience a different kind of life—the life God actually intended for them to live.

This life—shaped by what God truly cares about—is one that most people would have trouble believing God desperately desires for them to live. It's the life they've always imagined in the one place they would never look.[6]

THREE STORIES

To be honest, I could write many more pages than you are about to read on the culture of God's kingdom revealed in the parables. As an exercise, our church staff spent several hours exploring all of the parables in Scripture and then writing on a whiteboard all of the kingdom takeaways from them.[7] We studied every parable Jesus taught, discussed them in groups, shared major takeaways, and then summarized the key cultural message. For each parable, we were instructed to fill in the blank at the end of this sentence: "This parable reveals a culture of _____."

What we discovered changed us as a church staff, changed me as a pastor, and changed how we lead and curate the culture of LifePoint Church.

Astoundingly, all of the takeaways from each of the parables were positive. Nothing was negative. In fact, even when there were pronouncements of judgment, they were because various characters in the stories were overtly ignoring the goodness of God reflected in the narrative. And since these are stories, every listener is invited to see the ways they can avoid missing the positives of the kingdom.

The whiteboard filled up with words that characterize the culture of Christ's kingdom. And to the point of this book, they should characterize the churches we serve. I encourage you to do your own study of the parables and make your own list—and realize that these terms are what Jesus would use to describe the climate of the communities of his people. Among many others, our list included words like these: freedom, forgiveness, peace, excitement, persistence, deliverance, engagement, selflessness, faithfulness, creativity, redemption, invitation, acceptance, readiness, healthy, strong work ethic, wide nets, confidence, nonjudgmental, celebration, transparency, justice, grace-filled, and so many more. I remember stepping back to look at the whiteboard, and I began to pray that God would allow LifePoint Church to be a church that had a 100 percent positive culture like the kingdom of heaven!

These are the building blocks of the culture of God's kingdom. When I think about this, my mind can't help but move toward the concepts of building and construction. The journey we are about to take together will be just that: a building project. My desire is that we will take the materials of our own experiences, stories (both good and bad) from our churches, practical and philosophical insights, and stories and principles from Scripture to frame up new rooms in our hearts and minds.

Just as three-story houses provide more room for more people to stay, there are three main parables from Jesus (among all the others we should keep studying) that I want to focus on: the parable of the two sons, the parable of the sower, and the parable of the talents. I will also tell stories of more friends like Blane, real individuals who are experiencing things about God and his church that most people would never expect.

I will talk about individuals, but I will also talk about the church—yes, both. People tend to freak out about this distinction between the two. They want to know if this is a "personal growth" thing or a "church growth" thing. Honestly, many people today can't conceive of the fact that something can work on both a personal and a church level. Moreover, people who think they want something for their personal growth often avoid picking up something they think is for church growth. This contrived mutual exclusivity between personal and church growth is contributing—if not creating—many of the issues people and churches are experiencing. When we act as if they are separate, we reinforce a silly yet openly accepted idea: the real church is not made up of real people. Isn't that the very problem most people have with church in the first place? Why are we going along with it?

When we act as if the principles that will revolutionize an individual's life won't do the same for a community of individuals, we deny the very essence of all the things culture actually is. Culture is not a thing unto itself; it is a thing that results from the philosophies, patterns, belief systems, and behaviors of many people together. This is a book about aligning our versions of these things with Christ's.

The way to affect culture is to affect people—even a single person. So these stories will affect you on both a personal and a community level. Simply put, you can't really experience the fullness of the life for which you are created on a purely personal level that excludes the community around you. Being a self-sufficient loner or an expert who "takes care of my own business" sounds impressive, perhaps even noble and responsible. But in the end, even Wyatt Earp needed Doc Holliday.[8]

Finding fulfillment just for yourself sounds like what everyone in this world is searching for, but life just doesn't work that way, even though we act as if it does. This is why everything we will explore about community—and specifically the church—actually applies to you individually. Conversely, everything we will explore about you also applies to the church. You may see yourself and the church—for better or for worse—in every character in these stories:

> In a *son* who comes to his senses and comes home to the arms of a loving Father.
>
> In an older *sibling* who just can't celebrate the homecoming of his long-lost brother.
>
> In a *field* where different types of soil need to be turned over differently.
>
> In a *farmer* who makes room for a little seed to survive and grow.
>
> In a *master* who entrusts his amazing treasure to each of his servants.
>
> In a *miser* who refuses to rightly use what has been entrusted to him to steward.

In these stories, let's explore what God cares about deeply and what life in his kingdom—and his church—really feels like.

PART 1

THE PARABLE
OF THE
TWO SONS

CHAPTER 2

LOST THINGS MATTER

The Heart of the Father:
Turned toward the Missing

This is not a book about me—not in the least. But I do feel compelled to open up my heart and offer you a small glimpse into my own story so you will understand some of the reasons I see the world—and the church—through my particular lenses. After all, we all come from somewhere, and where we come from, what we've seen, and what we've experienced are all critical factors that, like it or not, shade our viewpoints of where we're going, what we're seeing, and what we're experiencing now.

I grew up in New Orleans and Shreveport, Louisiana, until I was about ten years old. My mom and dad divorced before my second birthday, so I have no memories of a family with two parents. I do, however, have many strong and fond memories of a mother who worked hard for her three sons. I was the youngest of this trifecta of rambunctious boys whom my mother had to chase around mostly by herself. She worked two jobs until I was about fifteen, so as you can imagine, she was very busy and tired all the time. Yet she never failed to ensure that we were able to play sports or do anything else we needed to do. She was my hero.

Apparently my parents had been regular church attenders

before their divorce, but that was not a reality I was aware of until much later. Still, it provided roots to fall back on throughout my life. For several years after the divorce, we were in and out of churches here and there. We were not antagonistic toward church; we were just trying to survive. All of that changed when we landed in a certain church, where we began going every Sunday morning, Sunday night, and Wednesday night.

It was a Holiness church, the kind where foot washings were common, where women didn't cut their hair or wear makeup, and where all the men wore suits all the time. The leaders of the church promoted an insular culture, trying hard to remain separate from the world outside the doors of the church.

It seems more obvious to me now than it did then that our family didn't fit the culture of this particular church. My mom was a working professional, serving as a social worker in clinical settings. She wore makeup and kept her hair cut short to help with ease of managing family and work. She also wore a professional suit almost every day, far removed from the attire of most of the women in that church who wore skirts that touched the floor.

But as is the case in any church or organization, relationships were the key. An older lady named Charlene had taken our family under her wing. She loved us dearly and became a spiritual mother to my mom and a spiritual grandmother to the rest of us. The thing I remember the most about Ms. Charlene was that she always gave us little hard candies called Coffee Nips. (I'm pretty sure there is an age minimum of eighty-five to buy them —of course, only under the condition that they will be given to little kids.) We called them coffee candy, and they were our favorite part of sitting through services.

We sat with Charlene in the second row every service, right behind the pastor and his wife. Charlene would sit on our left near the center aisle, and we would pile in beside her. The worship was demonstrative, with singing, dancing, and shouting—a classically charismatic environment. I don't remember thinking much about those kinds of things, the things most of today's church research and statistics focus on. For me as a kid, this was just our church, and it felt nice to belong somewhere. I did not realize at the time that our family was looked at by some of the congregation as something of a project.

My brothers and I were eleven, nine, and seven years old. I was the youngest. I guess you could say my brothers and I were normal kids who engaged in normal 1980s kids' things: *The Goonies*, Rubik's Cubes, *The Legend of Zelda*, fighting, being dumb—and of course, skateboarding.

One Sunday night as we sat in the service, one of my brothers was looking through the pages of a Tony Hawk skateboard magazine. If you're a parent, you know there are seasons when you look for *anything* to keep your kids quiet in church. So he sat there quietly flipping through pages, not making any sort of ruckus or distraction.

What happened next has never left me. The pastor stopped his sermon and turned his attention to my mother. "Ms. Burnette, you and your boys need to get on out of here," he said. "You can come back when you get your act together and are ready to live like the rest of us." We looked at each other in shock, but he wasn't joking. A long and uncomfortable silence ensued. Finally, Mom did what he asked, rummaging through her things to get everything together so we could leave—from the front of the church, no doubt. The pin-drop silence seemed to amplify every shuffle and sniffle as we took our walk of shame past the entire church to the back door.

As we walked out, no one else from the church walked out with us. No one stood up and protested that we were being kicked out. No one said, "Hey, Pastor, this is a young family with a hardworking mom doing the best she can, holding down two jobs and then rushing here every chance she can, just trying to keep her family in church. Maybe you should give them a break!" Nothing. No one came to our defense. No one spoke to us, much less for us. We left alone in silence.

I felt the same feelings as if I had been called to the principal's office (which was a regular occurrence until about eleventh grade)—shame, guilt, regret. But even at seven years old, I knew in my heart of hearts that something wasn't right about this. It is something our family has never forgotten. Even now as grown men, my brothers and I can recall that story. Fortunately we laugh about it now. But it's far more tragedy than comedy.

As an adult, I can't imagine what my mother must have already been dealing with during that time in her life: juggling two jobs, three boys, and the pressure of it all. But it's even more difficult to imagine what she must have felt when we were thrown out of Jesus' community because we didn't look the same, act the same, or measure up to the same "holy" standard they had somehow agreed was God's standard.

I've shared this story with my church before, and it always raises the ire of people who have endured similar experiences. Even now, I write this with tears in my eyes. When my family felt lost, the church told us to get lost.

REFLECTIVE CULTURE

This experience reinforced to our family something I think many people in this world think about God and his church: people who feel lost don't matter that much to them. When I became a pastor of a church, I told Stephanie, my wife, I would like to lead a church that would have never kicked me out. I know that sounds like an unorthodox motivation, but orthodoxy itself should never be separated from the basic, invitational premises of the gospel revealed in the life and teachings of Jesus. In other words, we shouldn't sing about amazing grace when we have little of it for those who don't look like us.

To that end, we even have a small group in our church that focuses on helping people survive and heal from past "church hurt." I want to lead a church where unchurched people can know beyond any shadow of a doubt that they are coming home to the Father and his family, where they'll never feel rejection from the insiders. I like to tell the folks at LifePoint, "Anyone is welcome to come and be a part of LifePoint Church and have their lives wrecked—turned upside down and transformed by Jesus, not wrecked by *Jesus' people!*"

Yes, there should be truth telling and disciple making in our churches. But if we elevate issues like makeup, magazines, or music above the grace-filled invitation of the real gospel or the God-breathed value of broken people, we're miles away from the culture of Christ's kingdom (and we can forget about making real disciples).

Whether we like it or not, our heavenly Father cares about lost sons, lost daughters, and missing persons (the outsiders), while older brothers (the insiders) tend to care more about themselves, even if they don't realize they are doing so.

I know my childhood story may seem extreme to you, and it may very well be such. Most kids reading skateboarding magazines would not be kicked out of most churches in the middle of most sermons. But let me ask you a question: Regardless of whether someone is actually thrown out of your church, is your church—the one you pastor or the one you attend—a place where lost people feel drawn in as if they have found their way back home? Just ask anyone who has ever sat through an uncomfortable Thanksgiving dinner with hostile relatives—you don't have to be thrown out in order to not feel invited in.

It's always interesting to read the setup of many of the parables, including the parable of the two sons. Jesus was being insulted and castigated by religious leaders because "outsiders" were longing to hang out with him. Even more, Jesus was longing to hang out with them as well. And the religious ones—the "holy rollers"—hated them and hated him for it. I love that outsiders are immensely attracted to Jesus. It is a shame that outsiders tend to be repelled by those who think themselves to be holy. More on that below.

Sometimes I ask pastors I speak to and coach, "Would your church be the kind of church that Jesus himself would want to pastor? Would it be the type of church where, if Jesus started preaching and leading alongside you, outsiders and sinners would flock to it? Or would they be rejected by the ones who are already following Jesus?" Here's another way to look at this: If Jesus were to interview for the senior pastor job and was able to attend services, interview members, visit several small groups, and generally immerse himself in what your church is saying, doing, attracting, and elevating as important, would he find it to be a place that meshes well with the culture reflected by his own words, actions, values, and ethics? Would Jesus fit in at his church that you pastor?

To be clear, I'm not talking about seeker sensitivity—that is, altering culture in purely superficial ways to the extent that it becomes hard to tell any difference between a church and one of the local nightclubs, country clubs, or workout clubs. Nor am I talking about simply changing our Christian terminology and delivery in such a way that our words and message become scarcely recognizable as Christian in an effort to be a softer version of the exact culture the world is already mastering better than we ever could. By the way, no one is so gullible that they don't realize they are coming to a church at 10:00 a.m. on a Sunday morning, no matter what you call it or how much smoky haze you pump into your professionally stage-lighted room.

Just as the parable below is a tale of two brothers, the concept of "church" is a tale of two cultures—or perhaps a tale of a million cultures versus one divine culture. I'm not talking about aesthetics, speaking styles, musical genres, or clothing; I'm talking about a culture where the heart of the Father is shared by those who live under his care—and specifically, what this kind of culture communicates to those who feel far away and have been told to "get lost" by the church.

A church with an attractive building and giftings can hide a culture within that is downright ugly, repulsing those who are looking for a place not just to belong but also to grow and be changed. But when the heart of the Father is rightly expressed, there is nothing more appealing or effective. Nothing we do should be done at the expense of the Father's culture. Our job is to make sure we understand the Father's heart and then craft our cultures to reflect his. That begins by understanding the first basic value found in the culture of the Father: lost things matter to him.

INSIDERS AND OUTSIDERS

Uncle Tom's Cabin was a revolutionary story written during a time when tensions had reached a fever pitch between the slave-owning South and the slave-free North. The story reflected the events that were happening around it. The same principle rings true for the writing of *Fahrenheit 451* as a reaction to the 1950s era of McCarthyism and Harper Lee's *To Kill a Mockingbird*, written during the civil rights movement of the 1960s. Although this is true of all books to some extent, the point is especially clear with these examples: the key to understanding these stories' themes and impacts lies in understanding what was happening when they were written.

The parable of the two sons in Luke 15 has probably shaped my understanding of the heart of God as it relates to the local church more than any other teaching of Jesus. To help us get the most out of this parable, we need to understand where Jesus was, who was around him, and what was going on when he told this story. It was an allegory that Jesus offered in the moment, bringing correction to some but throwing wide open the doors of hope to so many more.

Jesus was making his way up to Jerusalem. Along the way, the crowds of people following him began to notice the strangest thing about this person they knew was closer to God than anyone else they had ever seen or even heard of: he spent time with the people who were furthest away from God. He spent time with those who didn't exactly look like, act like, or fit in with the religious types of the day: "Now the tax collectors and sinners were all drawing near to hear him. And the Pharisees and the scribes grumbled, saying, 'This man receives sinners and eats with them.'"[1] We may not use the terms *tax collectors* and *sinners* very often these days, but they were significant labels in Jesus' time.

The bottom line was that the religious people of the day were mad at Jesus because of the company he was keeping. It was a bad look for such a good dude. Maybe you've experienced the anger of religious people too. Take it from a guy who was kicked out of church. It ain't fun or pretty.

But the crazy thing about Jesus was not just that he was hanging out with the religiously undesirable of that society; it was that those people actually *wanted* to hang out with him—they were "drawing near" to him. Doesn't this tell us something significant about Jesus? What an encouragement to faith leaders—pastors, missionaries, evangelists, leaders of Christian organizations! Can we plead with the Lord to help us become the type of ministers to whom outsiders and the "missing persons" in our towns are constantly drawing near? That's the type of church I truly believe we should be!

Before we begin to judge the religious people too harshly, as if they're just being mean to a bunch of misunderstood but still basically decent people, we should probably take some time to understand who Jesus was choosing to eat dinner with. Tax collectors were Jewish people who had accepted jobs working for Rome, the nation brutally occupying their country, to unfairly tax their Jewish neighbors so Rome could build more roads, temples, and shrines to pagan gods and elaborate homes and palaces for their leaders. And it gets worse. These tax collectors were notorious for extorting their fellow countrymen and keeping a cut of the profits, which, of course, the Romans didn't care two hoots about. Not only were they supporting the Jewish people's mortal enemy, but they were also making a killing in the process.

To the Jewish people—and probably to you as well if the same situation were to exist in your life—the tax collectors were nothing less than scumbags, traitors against the Jewish people and the Jewish ways. It wasn't just the religious elite who couldn't stand them; it was everyone else too. Imagine an IRS agent who cheats widows, overcharges and extorts small businesses in order to pocket the excess, and sells secrets to terrorists on the side. That's a modern-day equivalent of the tax collectors. They were the ultimate outsiders.

The Pharisees and scribes, on the other hand, were people you would probably be impressed with. They had high pedigrees of theological training and rigor. These guys literally memorized the entire first five books of the Old Testament. Have you ever tried just reading through the book of Numbers? They memorized it. While the Pharisees had God's Word committed to memory, the scribes were elevated Pharisees who handwrote copies of these memorized Scriptures.

Pharisees and scribes were the kind of people on guest lists; tax collectors and sinners were the kind of people on watch lists. The former would be candidates being interviewed for your local HOA; the latter would be suspects being interviewed by the FBI. We tend to look down on the Pharisees now, but in that day, you would probably pull over to check on them if they were broken down on the side of the road, while you would probably lock your doors at a red light if a tax collector was on the adjacent sidewalk.

Needless to say, the insiders looked down on the outsiders. But the outsiders weren't paying much attention to the insiders because they were mesmerized by Jesus. But Jesus, who you might expect to be the ultimate insider, didn't join in with the disdain against the undesirables. In fact, he seemed to actually enjoy their company, and they enjoyed his in return. It was a complete mystery and an offense to everyone who cared about what was right—or at least *who* was right. Honestly, it's still offensive today to those who think they care about what is right.

Thankfully, Jesus decided to set us all straight on what truly matters to him. He did this by telling a series of stories, each about lost things. The first is the parable of the lost sheep in which a good shepherd is willing to leave his ninety-nine sheep in order to go as far as possible to find the one that is missing. Jesus followed up this story with the parable of the lost coin in which a person is willing to flip all of the contents of her house upside down in order to find one missing coin, even though she may already have other jars full of sorted and counted coins.

But the third story is where I want to focus our energies, on a parable about a lost son.

The thing is, though, it's about more than just the one son who loses sight of what's important to his father. Both sons in the story blow it, and both need grace, but only the younger brother realizes it. Ironically, the older brother claims to be most concerned about what the father cares about, but he can't see that he is rejecting what is most dear to the father—the other son, his own brother.

As Pharisees and scribes gathered around Jesus in the presence of tax collectors and sinners, the stage was set for quite the story, and it was easy for everyone listening to the parable to know which characters represented themselves. Consequently, I believe the attitude of the older brother is still most often overlooked in our modern readings of this story—and it's still the attitude that surfaces most often in many churches, keeping us from being a place that feels like home to those who need to find their way to a place of forgiveness, healing, restoration, and purpose.

THE PRODIGAL PLOT THICKENS

If you own a Bible, this story from Luke 15 may have a header title of "The Prodigal Son." The word *prodigal* has become common in church culture; in fact, it is one of those rare terms that has been used so much in church circles that it has spilled into the larger, secular culture as well. The result is that most people think they know exactly what a prodigal is—a person who is backslidden, wayward, fallen from grace, sinful, and, above all else, deserving of being and remaining on the outside.

But Jesus didn't title the story when he was telling it. He just told a story.[2] Here's how it went.

There was a father who had two sons, and the younger son made a series of bad decisions. The first bad decision was coming to his father to ask for his share of the family inheritance. Then, as now, an inheritance typically only came after a parent had died, but this son had no desire to honor that natural process. He didn't want to wait around, work honorably for the family's name and advancement, care for his father in his old age, and then inherit his portion nobly so he could continue their collective legacy. He wanted out, and he wanted out right now.

We are familiar with the concept of inheritances in our time, so even to us, this seems like a lowdown request by the younger son. In ancient times, the custom was that after a father died, all his assets would be divided into equal shares determined by the number of children he had, plus one. Then the oldest son would get two shares while the other children would get a single share. So if you had five sons, you would divvy up the inheritance into six portions, and the oldest son would get two shares (known as a double portion), while everyone else would receive only one.

How hurtful the request must have been to the father! In essence, the younger son was saying, "I wish you were dead. I don't want to do life with you anymore. Can I just get what's coming to me and be done with this whole family?" As a dad, I can't imagine the pain and anger such a request—really, a demand—would produce in me. I imagine I would have some carefully selected words for my wayward kid that would help her (I only have daughters) understand her place.

But the father in the story Jesus told chose a different word: *Yes.*

Again, Jesus used parables to reveal key aspects of God's character and kingdom, so this part of the story reveals so much. The picture Jesus paints of this particular father is one who, out of love for his misguided son, allows his son to opt out of a relationship with him. He doesn't force the issue, though he certainly could have. Instead, he loves his son enough to let him make his own choices in this matter.

I don't think most people see this aspect of God as a loving characteristic. He allows us an incredible amount of freedom, which we often use to selfishly bypass his ways as we meander toward what we think will be better—that is, following our own ways. As a dad with daughters, I have to say that such a parental move would be hard for me to stomach.

Yet this dad honored his son's dishonorable request. In fact, Luke 15:12 implies that he didn't just give the younger son his single portion; he went ahead and gave the older brother the double portion he was going to receive someday in the future. It was a big day on the farm, and everyone got a lot richer—everyone except the father. He was about to lose what was much more important to him than assets or inheritances.

We don't have a record of how old these guys were supposed to be in the story, but I imagine they were intended to be somewhere in their mid to late teens or early twenties, since Jewish boys were considered to be men at the age of thirteen. Obviously, it's not apples to apples to compare a seventeen-year-old in ancient times to seventeen-year-olds today, but it's probably safe to say the younger brother was barely growing facial hair when he suddenly came into a fortune. Yes, it was only a third of his father's inheritance, but as the story later reveals, his father was beyond loaded—like multimillionnaire loaded.

All that money immediately began burning a hole in the younger son's pocket. He saddled up his newly bought, tricked-out camel named Ferrari and sped out of town without a look back toward his father and his childhood home. Little did he know that as he left, his father was standing in the field watching him leave and that each and every day after that sad day, the father would stand in that same field watching the same horizon where his younger son had disappeared, just waiting and hoping to see him crest the distant hills on his way home. The younger brother seemingly had no idea who his father was. (As it turns out, he wasn't the only brother who didn't fully know who his father was.)

Jesus continued the story by saying that the younger son "took a journey into a far country, and there he squandered his property in reckless living" (Luke 15:13). In other words, he immediately got busy doing everything his youth and fortune would afford him—and now he could afford a lot. You have to admit, it kind of makes sense. He was a teenager with a blank check. What would you have done if you were his age and walking around in his sandals? Most seventeen- or eighteen-year-olds who came into that much money would probably blow it in Vegas, on cars, in some sports gambling scheme. And let's be honest, you don't have to be a teen to make bad choices with money.

To that end, if we put aside our previous assumptions that the younger son was older and should have known better, we can more easily understand the word Jesus used to describe the way the young man lived. The original Greek word, *asōtōs*, is translated by some versions of the Bible as "prodigal." This translation would be accurate, except, as I referenced before, we have hijacked the word *prodigal* to mean all things sinful and evil. This particular Greek word only occurs one time in the entire New Testament, so we don't have other biblical contexts to compare it to. But as the ESV translates the word, a more effective definition for the modern mind would be "reckless."[3] Other helpful definitions would be "wasteful," "lavish," or "flagrant." No, these terms are still not necessarily the best labels to describe the way people should live their lives, but they are a little more accurate than our modern perception of the word *prodigal*. This will be an important point later in the story, both for those who originally heard Jesus tell it and for those of us who hear him tell it today.

It's common today to skip over huge parts of a story simply by saying, "To make a long story short . . ." That's basically what Jesus did when he said that the son squandered everything. We want details here, but Jesus left them out, choosing not to elaborate on the bad choices and wasteful decisions of the younger son. Jesus kept the boy's story simple: he rejected the father, took a bunch of stuff, left the father's presence, and squandered his life.

In not much time at all, the younger son singlehandedly lost everything he owned, blowing a fortune in a season of life before most of his actual life had even started. Imagine his dismay when he realized he just burned up his own safety net playing with fire—a safety net that was meant to keep him secure as a young man, a husband, a father, and eventually an old man. Almost as quickly as he had demanded his inheritance, he squandered it on lavish living.

But it got worse.

A severe famine hit the land. Jesus' audience knew this language well, since famine played a significant part in the history of the Jewish people, as evidenced by the Old Testament narrative.[4] Seasons of famine had often been seasons of divine provision for them; after all, when they had no one else to depend on, they realized their dependency on their Father.

It drove the younger brother to do the same, but not before he hit rock bottom, which, for a Jewish man, would be working with what their sacred law considered to be the most unclean of animals—pigs. The young man was not raised to be a fan of bacon, barbecue ribs, or pork belly; nevertheless, it was his belly that was the problem. So he did the unthinkable for a rich Jewish kid. He approached a local pig farmer and begged for a job, any job.

The farmer hired the recent washout to wash out his pigpens and feed his swine—a job most of us today would also acknowledge to be a dirty one. The Pharisees and scribes would have cringed at this part of Jesus' story. It was scandalous and shameful—and Jesus aimed to describe it that way. I think it's hilariously brilliant that Jesus made the pig farm a part of the story. Of course, we have the benefit of hindsight and know the way the story goes (probably), but the religious leaders did not. They were hanging on every word, no doubt becoming more and more convinced of the tragedy that was this young man's complete worthlessness.

The story was meant to provoke the religious holy rollers—to ensure that they were fully disgusted with the young man in the story. Jesus told them the young man had become so desperate that he spent some time fantasizing about diving headfirst into the pig slop so he could fill his belly with the leftover pods they were eating. That was it. The kid was off the reservation with no hope of returning. The story would have been more than effective to seal the fate of the young man. To the Pharisees and scribes, he was a lost cause, a wasted life, a disgusting and unholy disgrace to his father. And he was getting what he deserved. Little did they know that to the father back home, his son was lost, but he was not a lost cause.

COMING TO ONESELF

The seventeenth verse of Luke 15 is probably my favorite one in the whole story. It speaks of something I have watched occur in the hearts of "prodigals" so many times over the years. It is something that once happened in my heart when I was far away, covered in mud, and settling for deluded visions of pig slop.

Verse 17 reads, "But when he came to himself . . ." What a simple, beautiful, profound phrase from the mouth of Jesus.

He was describing an aha moment that he knew is possible in the heart and mind of every reckless, lost child out there. Jesus was pointing to a sudden moment of clarity in the heart of the son. This was the moment when the love of his father won him over—when the memory of how good his father had been to him overwhelmed his own sense of how far he had gone and how bad he had been. This was the moment when, even from a great distance, the overwhelming reality of the father's love penetrated the underwhelming reality of his own selfish pursuits. He knew his best and only option was to get back to his father.

And the most amazing aspect of this "coming to himself" moment was that, for the first time in this entire story, he changed his focus from himself to the father. Yes, he still was thinking about what he had to have to survive, but he stopped entertaining the idea that he could survive on his own. Instead, he remembered his father. He said to himself, "How many of my father's hired servants have more than enough bread, but I perish here with hunger! I will arise and go to my father."

People in every community today are living squandered and reckless lives, eyeing the pig slop before them and realizing their dire situations. They are hopeless. They have come to the end of themselves, which means they have also reached the moment of greatest potential to actually *come to themselves*. I'm convinced that God is drawing people to himself, and the spark of the whole process is the same moment the younger son experienced. This is where hope enters in and people realize there has to be a better way to do this life. The hope given by the Father is that moment when they finally stop thinking about themselves long enough to remember that even the most basic of lives under the love and in the community of the Father is infinitely better than the lives they are experiencing.

The desperation of the younger brother's situation caused

him to remember the goodness of his father—a goodness he knew he had rejected and taken advantage of. This is a theology that many people get so wrong that it does great damage to their perception of God. The truth is, God does allow and use hardship to teach or remind us of his goodness, but always for the purpose of drawing us back to him. Take note that the greedy request and the lavish, wasteful journey of the younger son were not the father's idea or doing—it was all the son's. Likewise, when we face hardships in this life related to our bad choices, if we can come to ourselves, we will realize that the father did not just drop us in the pigpen out of spite or even to teach us some cosmic and cruel lesson. It is all us.

Early in the story, it appeared that the younger son didn't know his father very well. After living with him for somewhere between one and two decades, he still wanted to leave the safety, provision, and relationship of life with his dad and his brother. But at this point, it becomes more apparent that some impression of the father's true nature had been successfully planted in the son's heart. When he finally came to his senses, he knew beyond the shadow of a doubt that any kind of life *near* his father was infinitely better than the one he had crafted and crashed on his own.

I love what happened next. This young man couldn't have been more nonreligious in his attitudes and actions up to this point in the story, but suddenly he crafts a three-point sermon he plans to deliver to his father. I bet he even alliterated the points in Hebrew. He began rehearsing his humiliating homily, and he had quite a bit of time to get it just perfect because, after all, he had a long journey from a distant, foreign land to get back home. I'm pretty sure this sermon didn't allow for time worked into the outline for taking up an offering or ending with a soft keyboard solo behind the invitation. It was raw and real. It reflected what "coming to himself" really entailed.

His first point focused on owning his mistakes and repenting of them: "Father, I have sinned against heaven and before you" (Luke 15:18). As a Jewish boy, he knew he had broken the fifth commandment—"Honor your father and your mother"—so he wanted to acknowledge his sin not only against his father but against God as well. The kid who had wanted so badly to own every ounce of value to which he felt entitled was now willing to own every ounce of shame for which he had exchanged it all. He set out to never be broke, but found himself utterly broken—and his delusions of grandeur were permanently gone.

Second, he planned to renounce his personal worth to the family as a son and a sibling: "I am no longer worthy to be called your son" (Luke 15:19). He intended to beat them to the punch—beating himself up before anyone else could. There would be no elephants in the room because before attempting to enter his father's house, he was going to bring the elephant along with him and position himself directly under its backside, letting it crush his reputation under the weight of his seemingly unspeakable shame before anyone could get a word in edgewise. Renouncing his worth made sense; he probably figured other members of his family had already done it anyway. (He was right.)

His closing remarks were simple: "Treat me as one of your hired servants." He was going to attempt to work his way back into some sort of second-class relationship with the father and the family, as if he were no longer even a blood relative. They would never have to worry about him demanding anything from them ever again, or even embarrassing them in front of the towns-people. He would forever wear the dishonorable title of "Black Sheep" with no qualms or resistance. He no longer wanted to live the high life. He was more than happy to settle for just a life, as long as it was at his father's place.

This is often the attitude of those who have lived life away from the Father, and it's one that we within the church often miss because we support it by our attitudes and actions. When people are desperate to return to the safety of God's love for them, they try to edge just a little closer to things related to him—usually by sneaking into the back row of a church or dropping in without drawing attention. They just want to be back in the room again, hear songs that tell of God's love for the lost, hear stories about a God who saves wretches like them. Just get in the room, get near the Father—not claiming any ground, but just claiming a seat.

They come with a sense of worthlessness, usually coupled with a desire to work their way back into some kind of lower level of acceptance from God and his people. Humans tend to default to a desire to make amends for our wrongs, to take matters into our own hands in an attempt to restore something that has been burned to the ground. We scoop up piles of ashes in our dirty hands and say, "Don't let me bother anyone here. I'm going to do whatever it takes to turn these ashes back into wood and rebuild what I burned down. Just let me be quiet and maybe serve somewhere where I won't do any more harm—maybe on the janitorial staff."

The son carved out a plan. He had no doubt that the father would agree with him: he was worthless. In this sense, he still didn't fully know the father. He did consider him to be a merciful man; after all, he had hopes that, out of pity, his father would accept his declarations of worthlessness and feel assuaged by guilt to the point of letting the son work off his debts as a hired hand. Of course, the idea of a future at the family table was gone. And the idea of any sort of future inheritance was simply laughable.

Armed with an impressively religious sermon that probably sounded spot-on to the Pharisees—who, by this point, were captivated by Jesus' story—the boy was on a collision course with what used to be his home. He had *come to himself*, but he—along with all the Pharisees, scribes, tax collectors, and sinners—was about to discover what it means to *come to the Father.*

NOT WHAT YOU EXPECT

Little did the younger son know—and little did the others hearing the story know either—but the father had never stopped watching the horizon where his boy had sped off with a third of his treasure and a lot more of his heart. There was no telling how many long days in the sun the father had spent working in the fields, constantly looking toward the edges of his property, imagining what it might look like to see the distant silhouette of his boy coming back home.

He remembered the day his son was born, how precious his little boy was to him before he had ever made any decisions, right or wrong. He remembered when they had played games in the yard and how he had sprinted to him in the middle of the night after a bad dream left the boy screaming in terror. He had protected him and comforted him always, not because it was his fatherly duty, but because he adored his son. The son had forgotten so much, as children often do, but the father had forgotten nothing—including all the vows of love he had spoken over the child before he was even old enough to understand them.

Most people think that our heavenly Father is sitting on his great and unapproachable ivory throne, just waiting for us to claw our way to him, just waiting for lowly sinners to slither into his presence and take their medicine. But Jesus forever shatters this completely inaccurate viewpoint of the Father, revealing him instead as he is: a dad who is constantly looking to the hills, longing to see us coming back to him. He is looking to our hearts and inviting, "When are you coming? When are you coming?

When are you coming? When are you coming? Come on, son! Come on, daughter! I'm looking. I'm looking. I'm looking everywhere for you!"

Then one day, it happened. The father saw a silhouette while the son "was still a long way off" (Luke 15:20). When he saw his son, instead of anger, resentment, a desire for restitution, or anything else we envision he might feel, he welled up with emotion and reacted with compassion at the return of his son. And then he did something that no one—neither the son in the story nor the listeners to the story—expected: he took off running toward his long-lost son. The multimillionaire was in a dead sprint that was every bit as reckless as the way his boy had squandered away his inheritance, his dignity, and his family name.

In ancient contexts, old men didn't run; rather, they would send runners to do their bidding. But he gets to the boy before the boy could ever get to him. I'm sure the son was exhausted from the journey, probably a little fearful at first about who was running at him with such passion. Then he saw his dad's face. This was not what he was expecting.

He braced himself to start his prepared statement before his father could start the dad speech that was sure to come, but before he could say a word, his father embraced him. The kid smelled bad from homelessness and his long journey, probably still reeking of pig slop, but the father didn't seem to notice. He started to kiss this boy's face, just as he did when his son was a baby. The father was making quite the spectacle of himself—and it was obvious he couldn't care less. The Pharisees had to shudder a bit at this part. What an irreverent image of any respectable father, and even worse, of God the Father. This image didn't fit their supposedly holy standard. But like it or not, it was an accurate image of God the Father—they just didn't truly know him.

Even though the son was no doubt pleasantly surprised by

the initial reception he was receiving, he knew he still had to deal with the matter at hand. So he gently pushed his father away so he could look him in the eyes and deliver his three-point sermon. "Father . . ." A long pause ensued so he could try to contain the deep emotions of shame and regret. "I have sinned against heaven and before you." Another deep breath, fighting back the tears and the tightening of the throat, he said the hardest thing ever: "I am no longer worthy to be called your son."

His father stopped him on his third breath, not even interested in whatever speech the boy had written. The servants had no doubt noticed that their boss had sprinted to the outskirts of their property, so they had very likely run after him to see what was wrong. He turned to them and began joyfully barking orders as quickly as the thoughts came into his head. "Quickly! Bring the best robe and get my boy taken care of! Call a DJ and tell everyone about the huge party we are throwing tonight. For this son of mine was dead, and is alive again; he was lost, and is found!"

The story wasn't quite finished yet, but Jesus had made a clear point and had established an image of what it means to belong to the culture of his Father's kingdom in one of the most effective and striking stories ever told. It was revolutionary; it still is.

But it shouldn't be revolutionary for those who say they value everything the Father values. This should be the attitude, disposition, and general ethic of grace and generosity that characterize every member of the Father's family, those who say they are working on his behalf to accomplish his purposes.

I believe that most of the problems people have with God and church are due to the inaccurate, faulty, graceless viewpoints we have of the Father. We don't tend to believe, much less reveal, that the heart of a loving father is to keep his eyes up, looking for who is missing. Sometimes we get this right, but many times we don't celebrate well when lost children come home. If we're honest, we sometimes don't even know what it looks like to see a lost son or daughter show up. We're often not even really looking that hard for them, much less preparing a party for them. In my own life, I've been guilty of normalizing a new salvation or not stopping to celebrate that someone recently gave their life to Jesus. Worse, I've lost the excitement of someone coming to faith because of the other stressors of church or family life.

As the next chapter will unpack in greater detail, the father was the only one in the story who was looking up and watching for the prodigal's return. The thing was, the older brother had his head down, doing "good things" on the father's farm. As God's church, we should be reflecting his image, but we can easily become a faithful gathering of older brothers who do housework for the Father while completely missing the heart and passion of the Father's house.

The bottom line is that our Father cares about lost people, and if we walk in the attitude of the older brother in Jesus' story, we will only care about ourselves. This doesn't have to be so, as the father explains in the story itself, if we can only hear what is being said.

CHAPTER 3

THE FATHER'S ECONOMY

The Grace (Not Shame)
of the Loving Father

When it comes to people's perceptions of Jesus and his mission for coming to this earth, there is a movement afoot in many churches that likes to sum up his infinitely divine and eternally executed plan in terms that can simply sell the gospel a bit short. The fullness of the gospel of Jesus and the eternal plan of God's redemption and salvation is not easily summed up in a bumper sticker quote. The gospel is just so much more than "Jesus came to die for our sins." Yes, he did come to do this, and yes, the cross is the crux of the matter. But splattering this message on T-shirts, billboards, social media posts, and church marquees is not the same as fully communicating to the world the good news that Jesus came to proclaim and to fulfill. When we sum it up all too neatly, it may still sound like *good* news but may not come across as very *big* news.

Christ's mission, which is also now directly related to our mission as his church, was to reveal the heart of the Father to a world that wasn't sure he could be trusted. The Old Testament chronicled thousands of years of the epic struggle of people to meet the potential of their creational intention, along with the epic lengths to which the Creator went to bring them back into right relationship with him, which, consequently, was the centerpiece of their creational intention.

Promises made. Sin. Promises broken. A flood. A covenant of faith. Exile and slavery. A deliverer. A deliverance. Law. Wilderness. Promised land. Judges. Kings. Prophets. Exile. Promise of a new Deliverer. Then hundreds of years of prophetic silence.

The people continued to wait on the promised Messiah. Then he came, in the form of a person: Jesus himself. In him, the answer to this greatest question—can God be trusted?—was intended to be a painfully (especially for Jesus) obvious yes! God can and should be trusted. In fact, trusting God is the only path to real life, both in the present and in the eternal future. Jesus came to reveal that God is a merciful Father—so much so that he was willing to pay off the bill for every mistake made with the priceless currency of his own Son's life.

So you see, while there are still mysteries about God's sovereignty and his workings in history and eternity, Jesus came to clear up the mysteries about God's feelings toward us, as well as whether he can be trusted. That is the central premise of the gospel—not just *what Jesus did* on the cross but also *why he did it* and how he invites anyone and everyone into a place of full safety and security in eternal relationship with him.

And yet so many people, both inside and outside the church, like to make conclusive statements regarding their opinions of any and all other mysteries related to faith that they can think of . . . as if they have a fully irrefutable answer.

Age of the earth. Suffering in the world. Music or no music in church. Ways to guarantee answered prayer. What day to worship. Sprinkling or dunking. The meaning of biblical prophecy. Details about the end of the world. Versions of the Bible. How God's gifts work. What kind of Christian gets to heaven.

The result is that most of what we proclaim as the church is not the main thing Jesus came to proclaim: that God is good and can be trusted. We act as if speaking conclusively or leading boldly in areas related to all these other mysteries will somehow magically draw people into a truly transformative relationship with God. I'd venture to say they do not. Why? Because we're not prioritizing the mystery most people struggle with: *Is God trustworthy?*

We may not say it so bluntly, but we sure do live it bluntly. We say it by the way we are insecure in our own relationships toward God, either fearfully waiting for a divine lightning bolt to take us out when we make mistakes or, worse, making others whom we deem to be more "sinful" than us feel as if they are about to experience the bolt of God's wrath—yet we're the ones who usually end up bolting on those who most loudly question God's trustworthiness. We act as if we are in less need of grace than "them," whoever our particular "them" may be. Can't you see how we seem very confused about the things Jesus came to clear up, yet we seem very confident about so many things he was uninterested in completely revealing?

The answer to the question "Is God trustworthy?" is a resounding *yes*. And the way to help others understand this is to keep returning to the actual words and life of Jesus. If we will listen, we will discover that we can stop basing so much of the Christian life on things Jesus didn't address—things that don't bring life. More importantly, we can stop acting confused about God's nature and his attitude toward people. Instead, we can redirect our energies toward taking hold of the correct kingdom disposition that will create room for God to wreck people's lives in the most amazing and transformative way imaginable, in the way only God can.

I guarantee you that as the younger son was being kissed by

his dad, and as the servants were scurrying in and out of the scene bringing him new suits of clothes and trays of fresh delicacies, he was beyond wrecked—this was *not* what he expected his father to be like. But he was gloriously wrong.

So are we. Even so, the real good news says we don't have to stay that way. We can begin to expect, engage, and share the heart of the Father if we stop spending so much of our time and energies on the wrong mysteries, instead acknowledging and aligning ourselves with the divinely inverted value system—the *economy*, if you will—by which God lives and deals with people.

HE SAID, SHE SAID . . . BUT I SAY

As we are discovering with the perceptions of the Pharisees and scribes, as well as the tax collectors and sinners, Jesus' story of the two sons was nothing less than revolutionary. However, it wasn't any different from the message Jesus had been proclaiming throughout his ministry—and it certainly wasn't the first time he had said such scandalous things about the way God measures and weighs sinfulness, grace, and the value of his children.

Jesus talked this way all the time, but most people who came to hear him were somehow unable to really *hear* him—that is, to comprehend what he was really saying. Again, this is why Jesus often used parables—to continually reveal his Father's true message to a fallen humanity that somehow always finds a way to look down on someone else more fallen than themselves.

The parable of the two sons was merely an application of the gospel Jesus had been preaching the whole time. So before we continue on with this parable, it behooves us to take a brief look at one key feature of Jesus' most famous sermon.

His most famous public talk was called the Sermon on the Mount, mainly recorded in Matthew 5–7, as well as in Luke 6. This is where Jesus makes many famous statements about who is blessed, in a section sometimes referred to as "the Beatitudes." Others have written libraries of commentary and discussion about this amazing sermon, but we don't have time to explore every avenue of the content here.[1] I'd like to focus on a key phrase in Jesus' sermon: "You have heard that it was said . . . But I say . . ."

Jesus used this philosophical paradigm to approach a variety of topics, directly addressing the differences between the way most of us view other people and how to treat them versus the way God views people and desires that we treat them. It's a classic case of "he said, she said . . . but I say." These were direct statements of what Jesus values most and how it generally conflicts with what we value most.

These chapters of Matthew reveal a back and forth of this "you have heard that it was said . . . But I say . . ." technique. The previous chapter tells us that Jesus was traveling around all the various regions of Galilee, proclaiming and preaching "the gospel of the kingdom." This is significant. We often read phrases like "the gospel of the kingdom" in Scripture and chalk them up to flowery language or things we assume we already know. We overlook the significance of these terms because we're already familiar with them.

But Matthew is trying to tell us something, namely, that the "you have heard that it was said . . . But I say . . ." statements we are about to read in the chapters to follow were not just some collection of random, pseudospiritual sayings strung together like a stack of tiny papers from a divinely inspired box of fortune cookies.[2] They were not at all isolated observations recorded in Scripture to demonstrate just how mysterious and intellectual Jesus could sound. I'm afraid that's how we often treat these teachings, which is why we tend to dismiss most of what Jesus said in this sermon because it's just a little "too heavenly minded to be of any earthly good." Sure, loving your enemy *sounds* inspirational and stirring. But come on, no one *really* expects us to not repay those who hurt us with a little hurt of our own.

The truth is, this is exactly what the scriptural section heading "The *Sermon* on the Mount" suggests—it is supposed to be one cohesive sermon to apply to real life, not a loose connection of random philosophical sayings. Jesus is making points he intends to be interconnected, demonstrating what the gospel of God's kingdom (a real thing, not just a catchy-sounding concept) was really like. These are purposefully communicated concepts, the same ones Jesus had already been expressing as he had been traveling and teaching in all the synagogues in the surrounding geographical areas as referenced in Matthew 4.

Jesus' general takeaway for his listeners was something like this: "This is what you can expect life to be like when I rule as your King and you are gladly living in my kingdom." All of the topics he then discussed were the same ones about which all of his listeners already had opinions, beliefs, and practices— things about which they had "heard that it was said": lust, anger, marriage, sex, infidelity, betrayal, prayer, and many more topics.

In each case, Jesus demonstrated how the gospel of the kingdom would joyfully bring his values to bear on human life. It would be the revealing of a true kingdom life that would be infinitely fuller, eternally more significant, and strikingly more authentic and spiritual than the religiously flavored yet still untransformed lives everyone was currently living.

If there is a general tone and takeaway to this sermon and the technique Jesus uses, it has to do with our perception of how we treat people who are like us versus how we treat people who are not like us. Jesus cites examples about how natural it is for us to bless those who bless us—and, of course, to feel no obligation to bless those who persecute us. Hate our enemies, but love our friends. It only makes sense, doesn't it?

Jesus was homing in on the central ethic of the culture of his kingdom by juxtaposing it against the central ethic of the culture of the world, which is to accept those who fit in with you or your group and reject those who do not. As with many factors related to culture, we're often not fully cognizant of the effects or implications of the way we feel, believe, or act, especially when something has been the only norm we've ever known. It is like being born into a family that roots for the University of Alabama. You end up wearing crimson and cheering for a "tide" (which is like cheering for a wave, I guess?) just because your pappy did, as did his pappy before him. You just don't know any better. (A little fun here from a Tennessee graduate. Go, Vols!)

In all seriousness, Jesus' description of the culture of his kingdom would have felt totally foreign to his listeners. If we're honest with ourselves, it feels foreign to us. We simply feel pre-programmed to preserve and protect those who preserve and protect us and reject those who reject us. It seems to be as normal and familiar as the force of gravity or the sun setting in the evening.

But Jesus calls us to something different—to something higher. He calls us to a way of life and thinking that is not normal. His message is a reversal of the cultural impulses we know that draw us toward the insiders and repel us from the outsider. In his accounting, the values are reassigned. His evaluation metric has a different set of guiding principles and measurables. Remember, he's good and can be trusted, and he isn't just rigging the system with "gotcha" religion.

But this is how we often treat Jesus' kingdom message, as if he is just setting an insanely high standard that he never expects us to truly reach through belief, much less action. We act as if he is just trying to give us something impressively pious-sounding to reach for so we will become better than we were before, but fully knowing we can't really get there.

But what if he was serious? What if he really intended to change the economy of our natural souls, inverting the value system and exchanging the old ways for something eternal and seemingly foreign? Nah, that can't be it. Most of us treat his message more like a moral of the story from a 1960s TV show. Sure, it sounds good when Andy Griffith says it to Opie, but Christ's message that people have infinite value and should be loved with the same love with which he loves us is a little much, don't you think? Because if you really add it all up, people are only as valuable as their actions in relation to how said actions affect me.

And so we sum up, make T-shirts, post rhetoric to social media, and do anything else we can to make it *look like* we actually believe it—anything, that is, but *actually* believe it.

I think we sometimes water down Jesus' words and teachings because we misinterpret certain terms he used. Let me offer you one of my favorite examples. In Luke 14:26, Jesus says, "If anyone comes to me and does not hate his own father and mother and wife and children and brothers and sisters, yes, and even his own life, he cannot be my disciple." *Hate*? That's a strong (and seemingly sinful) word for a Christian to use, especially toward one's family.

The confusion arises over the word itself, but as biblical scholar Craig Keener points out, the word *hate* in this context can function as a hyperbolic, Jewish way of saying to "love less" or to "love secondarily."[3] Thus the word *hate* in the way Jesus uses it is more of a Jewish idiom than the literal way we use the word in English. Even so, we have a similar use of the word in our language that demonstrates what Jesus meant. Even though I live near Nashville, the home of the Tennessee Titans football team, I am from New Orleans, so I cheer for the Saints. If we were to get beat by the Titans, which is not very likely, I may say something like, "Man, I hate those Titans!"

But this doesn't mean I literally hate them. This does not mean I wish I could blow up Nissan Stadium or physically harm their players. It just means I don't like them as much as I like the Saints. I prefer the Saints, so I like the Titans *less*.

The idea that loving others less who are either not like you or simply don't like you is an acceptable attitude and practice is the real target Jesus is hitting with these comments. He is telling us, "You've always been taught by culture to love those who are like you and to love less—or not at all—those who are different from you."

Jesus is pointing out the common societal economy as we know it so we can understand what is so different about his economy. His point is that we should be people who not only love those who are easy to love or who don't offend us, but also be those who don't think it odd to absorb the offense and to love people for reasons other than mere human give-and-take. His revolutionary message is about loving those who don't give us good reasons to, who don't fit into our particular cultural milieu. In fact, his kingdom ethic is to love the very ones culture tells us to hate, and to love him even more than we love any of them.

The basic premise of most of our relationships is pretty simple: if you fit and you're like us, come on in. But if you don't fit and you're not like us, we should not feel obligated to care, much less love you. It's all a game of "them" versus "us," and since the whole world shares this perspective, it must be okay, right?

Jesus says his ways are different, and no character reveals the antithesis of his ways better than the one who should have been most excited to see the younger brother come home—his older brother.

AN EXTRAVAGANT FATHER
AND A STINGY BROTHER

Older brothers come in all shapes and sizes. As we do with many biblical characters, we like to peg them as monsters who were against everything Jesus stood for. Rogues. Villains. Bad guys who wanted nothing more than to take down the good guys.

But the truth is, most of us have at least a little bit of the "older brother" inside us—a "them" versus "us" mentality that surfaces if the conditions are just right. A certain kind of person crosses the white line into *our* lane on the interstate—or perhaps a certain kind of person crosses *our* racial or cultural border—and all of a sudden, our *Follow Me to Church* bumper stickers don't mean much. It's difficult to see this in ourselves because our known economy tells us such a mentality is more than fair—and that it is also normal, so it must be right. Right?

Jesus knew this, so in telling the story with an older brother, he painted perhaps the most masterful picture there is of the person we tend to become, the person who fills many of our churches.

To understand the older brother in the story, you have to go back to the father again because the father's actions initiate the entry of this final character. When you examine these actions, the term *embarrassment of riches* comes to mind. I know I brought this up in the last chapter, but let's play the scene out just a little longer. The father is so ecstatic about the return of his son that he can hardly get the words out fast enough. In a matter of minutes, he orders the entire house into the process of preparing a massive party.

Hey, you! Help my son find the bath so he can clean up—he's too good for this pig stench. And you, run as fast as you can and find the best robe in his old closet. Don't give him his brother's old, worn-out robe in the back of the closet that nobody wears anymore. I want him

*donning this year's latest fashion! And oh dear, look at your feet! They
are blistered! You, go get my boy a decent pair of shoes because he's home
now and he'll need to walk around here in comfort and confidence.
And, son, what happened to the old ring I gave you when you were
seven? You know what, it doesn't matter! You, go to my chambers and
get the gold ring from my bedside table and give it to him immediately—I think we're about the same ring size. And let's find the best calf
on the property and fire up the barbecue! My boy was gone, but he's
back now! It's like he was dead, but he's very much alive now!*

Man! I love this story! Can you not feel the father's giddiness?
It was electric, and the party was real. But is this how most people
feel when they try to crest the hill toward God by pulling their
car into a church parking lot? Yes, I know the sign reads, "Visitors
Welcome," but do they sense the giddiness of God when they are
trying to edge near to him?

The crazy thing about the father in the story is that he
is rich—very rich. As Tim Keller points out in his book *The
Prodigal God*, it is the father who now becomes wasteful.[4] That
was his economic philosophy—to keep spending. He had already
spent so much money when he allowed the son to leave, and then
even more time looking to the hill for his precious son. Now that
his greatest wish was coming true, he wasn't going to miss his
moment to keep spending lavishly!

But if we don't know and share the heart of the Father,
we can miss our moment. It really seems crazy to the natural
mind because his actions are seemingly unjust, at least as we
evaluate justice. The little scoundrel has literally squandered
his inheritance, fancy clothes, expensive rings, and his right
to ever again have even a birthday mini-cupcake with a single
candle, much less a full-blown bash the sounds of which could
be heard from miles around. Doesn't the father care about what
he had done?

And if you search your heart, you may find you are asking the same question: *Doesn't God care about what people are doing these days? Someone has to have standards around here, right? Why should we let people get away with that type of spoiled and lavish living?*

The father is the most offensive person in the story. He did not demand that the son "get his butt over here and kiss the ring." Instead, he kissed the kid and *gave* him the ring! He didn't meet him at the edge of the property, saying, "You've got a lot of nerve coming back here, so before you step foot on my farm, son, you better know you've got a lot of work to do to earn back my trust."

No, he was legitimately glad that the dirty, smelly, wasteful young man covered in pig feces was home. And you can't fake legitimate gladness. I have a feeling that many churches have tried and don't even know they've failed, especially as long as older brothers stick around and greet younger brothers as they make their way in. Like so many people who test the waters of coming back or coming to God for the first time, the younger brother came home with some serious baggage—regrets, addictions, patterns. But the father made it clear: "I don't care about any of that. You're home! You were dead, but now you're alive! That's all there is to talk about. Now, let's *party!*"

Really? Can it be that the father in the story doesn't care about those other things? Shouldn't he at least have mentioned the elephant in the room—that he didn't approve of his son's wasteful living? These seem to be fair questions, but they arise from our own twisted-by-sin sense of the concept of fairness itself, the one that blinds us to our own offenses and magnifies the offenses of others. We may not be as direct as the older brother, but we find ourselves just a little offended that the father wasn't more offended at his son's return.

But this offense within us seems to offend Jesus the most. It's why he told this story in the first place, curiously leaving out any semblance of a harsh word from the father to the younger son. Did the father care about right and wrong? Of course he did. It is ludicrous to think otherwise. But still, the conspicuous lack of even a mention of the boy's offenses was intentional—a grenade dropped into the mindset of everyone hearing the story, both then and now, who think they understand God and the way he looks at "bad" people. I mean, can you imagine being one of the scribes or Pharisees listening to this?

Jesus was continuing to invert their economy, showing them that they were flying upside down compared to the Father's heart. Or even better, can you imagine the hope rising in the hearts of every tax collector and sinner in the crowd? Jesus was adding fuel to the fire of excitement that was burning on the inside—a hope that perhaps life and faith as they knew it would be forever different. This was a consistent ethic for Jesus. Anytime he engaged a person who was living in habitual sin, caught in adultery, extorting others, full of greed, and the like, he consistently invited them to sin no more and follow him—*without* first demanding repayment for what they had done.

In the church world, we get so anxious about celebrating people who aren't like us. Jesus' economy from Matthew 5 freaks us out just a little too much. We still tend to love people like us and hate people different from us. We're really good at loving those people not like us less, whether because they are of a different race or a different denomination, or perhaps because they live on the other side of a border from us. Now, we'll do a missions trip into *their* land, but are we sure we want them to come into *our* land? We love people less who have different gender expressions or sexual orientations than we do.

But as the story reveals, the Father doesn't mention any of that, even though he certainly cares about those things—a lot, in fact. He just cares more about the people who have issues than he does about the issues people have. I referred earlier to the saying in our church: "Anyone is welcome at LifePoint Church to come and have their lives wrecked by Jesus." I'm a firm believer that Scripture is clear that God is in the business of wrecking our ever-so-wrong lives with grace and community until they become ever-so-right in ways we could never fathom, much less accomplish, on our own. God loves us just as we are, but he also loves us enough not to leave us that way.

This loving, real process of transformation is the main work of the Father, another expression of his grace. How tragic it is when people who are willing to come home are not allowed full access to the Father's property. The truth is, it's not really the Father's property we're worried about—it's ours.

Enter the older brother.

One has to ask, "Where has the older brother been throughout this entire story?" Doing what he was supposed to do, that's what—and don't you forget it! This guy was the rock of his father's farm, working long hours without ever giving a thought of leaving for greener pastures. He was the kind of person you would ask to house-sit for you while you and your family go on vacation (the younger brother was the one you would never dream of asking because of the potential for property damage from his wild parties).

Yet it is actually the father who was now throwing a wild party, and the older brother, tired from a hard day's labor out in his father's fields, trudged his way back home only to hear the thump of the pulsating bass line in the distance (so to speak).

Now his older son was in the field, and as he came and drew near to the house, he heard music and dancing. And he called one of the servants and asked what these things meant. And he said to him, "Your brother has come, and your father has killed the fattened calf, because he has received him back safe and sound." But he was angry and refused to go in. His father came out and entreated him.

Luke 15:25–28

Notice that the servant calls the other son "your brother," which will prove significant later in the story. Regardless, the older brother was furious and decided to try to shut down this ridiculous party for this wasteful son. It is the classic attitude of older brothers that not only tries to stop parties from happening when people come home to the Father but also keeps the older brothers from going to the parties themselves. Thus they miss out on the best part of the Father's work, the one that he wants to share with them more than anything that the fields of religion and church have to offer.

But the older brother was angry and refused to go into the party. His attitude came through loud and clear: "I'm not going in there with *him*!" It's the attitude of the group of people who kicked me out of church over a magazine. The idea sounds right—that is, fair. "I'm not doing life with them because they don't do life the correct way—the Father's way!" Historically, this is the way of religious people because we're good at loving people like us and hating people different from us.

We don't have any record that the older brother had the nerve to tell the servant to order the father to come out and see him, but we do have a record that he didn't go into the party. Somehow the message must have reached the father in the middle of his feasting and dancing. The message was clear: just outside the party tent, the older brother was ticked off and sulking.

Suddenly the one who seemed so righteously indignant toward the other son's disrespectful attitude toward the father had no qualms about brandishing his own version of disrespect.

Even more surprising is the lack of tension the older brother feels about this obvious contradiction. This is what happens when we embrace the attitude of the older brother—we somehow still think we're defending the honor of the Father, even as we dishonor the Father by refusing to obediently follow him into the work most dear to his heart—welcoming home our missing brothers and sisters.

The father was patient and gentle with the older brother, just as he was with the younger. He loved the older brother no less than the younger. Even when he was being mistreated yet again by one of his sons, he continued to function in his inverted economy of grace-based value over performance-based value. He had already dealt with the *lost* son; now he was dealing with the *self-righteous* son. Incidentally, both needed the father to change their lives. Both were sadly far from the father.

Think about it: the older son was as lost as the younger. He simply didn't realize it because he never left the farm. He stayed busy doing the work required to keep the fields in order. He never left, but somehow was still lost. He was close to the father's hand but far from the father's heart, and that's why he didn't think to approach the father with the same humility, repentance, and gratitude as his brother. He showed his true self—his rude, entitled, and vindictive self—all the while, claiming to be a faithful son who shared the values of a father he looked nothing like.

The father was lavishly paying grace forward to both sons, but the older brother wanted payback for all the crimes—perceived and actual—that his brother had committed. He did not want someone "not like him" invited to belong on the estate next to him with the full acceptance of the father and the family. He loved his brother less, despite the fact that his father insisted on loving him all the more.

CAMOUFLAGING

In the next chapter, we will explore the details of the older brother's tirade to the father, as well as the ways God's people should respond to all other people (who are also God's people) who are willing to come home to the Father's grace estate: the place of safety, community, forgiveness, transformation, and freedom that God desires for all his children, lost and found. But for now, let's button up these thoughts on the Father's economy with another story about being prepared to accept people who don't necessarily fit into our perfect box.

We have a man named Tracy in our church. He is a man's man, if you know what I mean. He loves hunting, fishing, and the outdoors. He's also a bit of a social introvert—that is, he isn't necessarily the kind of guy who wants to stand at the front door and endure introductory conversations with brand-new people. No, his best place is always in the great outdoors.

You never know what might be keeping people from cresting the hill and coming near to God. It's not always a story of riotous squandering. Sometimes the hesitancy arises from personal insecurity or a perception that they simply don't belong—that they are somehow a "them" and not an "us." This is why it's so important to understand the Father's heart for everyone and to establish a church culture that authentically reflects that heart.

Tracy believed this, so he was willing to be a part of something simple but crucial—the first impression someone has when they pull into the parking lot of a church. Yes, I know that "the church" is not our building, our campus, or even what happens on Sunday, so I'm not indicating that visitors who pull into our parking lot are exactly the same as the younger son walking back to the father's house. However, many people who are dragging a lot of hurt, baggage, misperception, and the like pull into a church parking lot, rehearsing all the conversations they expect to have with God and his people. Like the younger son, they usually expect a cold reception.

We do our best to change this way of thinking from the moment they approach our property, and Tracy was willing to help. As an avid hunter, Tracy is the kind of guy who wears camouflage as an everyday outfit. He doesn't need a camping trip as an excuse to deck out in full camo regalia. Every Sunday, Tracy is at the gate in hunting camo, waving as people enter the property.

On a cold, rainy spring morning, no one stood out better at the edge of our parking lot than Tracy in his full waterproof camo (with an orange vest, of course) to welcome newcomers with a smile and a wave. We also have a sign that directs first-time guests to flash their headlights at the parking attendant so they can be redirected to the first-time guest parking located steps from the building.

On this particular morning, a minivan flashed its lights, so Tracy flagged it down to give a welcome and to give the driver directions. To his dismay, when the man driving the van rolled down his window, he was laughing with his wife, trying to compose himself as Tracy gave his greeting and extended a handshake. As the laughter continued, Tracy worried this laughter was somehow directed at him, and it quickly became an awkward moment at the edge of the property.

"What are you laughing at, sir?" Tracy inquired as mildly as possible.

The man picked up on what was happening and said, "Oh no, man, I'm sorry. It's just funny to me that you're standing here in full camo."

This conversation wasn't getting any better. "Why is that funny?" Tracy asked.

"Well," the man continued, "my wife's been inviting me to

come to this church for weeks, and I keep finding excuses not to come. I just don't feel like I belong with these kind of people. I'm more of an introvert who likes to be outside. So I told her on the way here this morning that if I were to see other men here who are hunters, then maybe this whole church thing could work out for me. And wouldn't you know it, the first guy I see is you, standing at the front gate wearing full camo!"

What an incredible moment! The heart of the Father was to meet this young dad at the edge of this church property, ready to welcome him just as he was, even to affirm his own need to find a unique welcome to "The Father's House." The message of the gospel is what changes people's hearts, not what we wear, how we craft the order of our services, or how we structure our classes and small groups. Our job as those who live under the grace of the Father is to understand his heart for everyone who needs to come home. To be intentional about not being offended that God wants people who don't look like us, act like us, or share our exact value systems. In this case, on the outside Tracy did look like the man who was visiting—literally. The point really isn't what's on the outside, but rather what God is doing on the inside. The man was not where Tracy was in terms of trusting God and pursuing life with his people, and yet, even so, Tracy was ready to meet him where he was spiritually, even though they both happened to be wearing camo.

Being this kind of church means reversing our kingdom economy to value what the Father values. The heart of a loving father is to watch the hills, looking and longing for missing sons and daughters to come home; the heart of an older brother is to keep an eye on what they are doing, not paying attention to who is coming or going or caring about their return. The heart of a loving father is to operate from a context of forgiveness, grace, and celebration; the heart of an older brother is to operate from a context of shame, payback, and deception. The heart of a loving father is to throw lavish parties when lost sons and daughters come back home; the heart of an older brother is to throw a fit when those who seem like they don't belong are just trying to get home to their Father.

Everything God does toward us is motivated by his central ethic of generosity. If we want to be more like Jesus, generosity should be our central ethic too. Otherwise, we end up being older brothers who are not only displeased that certain kinds of people are finding the grace of the Father, but we also become those who miss out on the amazing party the Father is throwing—a party to which all of his children are invited. This party is supposed to be what "church" feels like.

CHAPTER 4

THROW A PARTY

The Father Throws Parties;
Older Brothers Throw Fits

Have you ever been in an argument with a family member or spouse when something slipped out that you never planned to say? Some people call this "word vomiting," and as the term suggests, it usually isn't a good or pleasant experience. However, it can be an honest experience and helpful in revealing what is going on inside your head and heart about a certain person or topic.

Jesus knew all about this experience, which is why he said, "Out of the abundance of the heart the mouth speaks."[1] He was reinforcing the truth that we can tell a lot about how we really feel and what we really believe based on what comes out of our mouths in conversations, *especially* when we are not planning what we are going to say.

As we return to the parable, this principle yields valuable insight into the "older brother attitude" that so often characterizes our churches. The older son was standing outside the party, refusing to come inside with his father and his brother—perhaps demanding to speak with his dad. His father leaves the party to try to reason with his son. The ensuing conversation unleashes a slew of words that is eerily reminiscent of the way many feel about God and church—and the way God is trying to change our hearts here to reflect the culture of his kingdom.

> But he answered his father, "Look, these many years I have served you, and I never disobeyed your command, yet you never gave me a young goat, that I might celebrate with my friends. But when this *son of yours* came, who has devoured your property with prostitutes, you killed the fattened calf for him!" And he said to him, "Son, you are always with me, and all that is mine is yours. It was fitting to celebrate and be glad, for this your brother was dead, and is alive; he was lost, and is found."
>
> *Luke 15:29–32, emphasis mine*

To begin, his whole speech has a real "look here, old man" feel to it. This speaks to the entitlement and disrespect referenced earlier, but it also speaks to the general older brother attitude that leads us to begin reading off our résumés to God as if he doesn't already understand our lives and, more importantly, what's best for our lives.

Had the older son been working faithfully for his father? We have no reason to think otherwise, but we do have reason to think this son didn't understand his father's heart. As he listed his accomplishments, it's obvious he believed two things: that the younger son did not deserve the party and gracious restoration he was receiving from the father, and that he himself deserved much more than this because of his work record.

Jesus deals with this concept a lot in Scripture—the restructuring of fairness along the lines of his grace rather than merit. It is also vividly revealed in Matthew 20:1–16, where Jesus tells another parable, this time about a master who hired laborers throughout the day at a certain agreed-on rate. As the day progressed, the master kept going into the marketplace and hiring more and more workers, which meant that some of them worked much shorter shifts than the ones who started in the early morning.

So when the day came to an end, the master paid all the workers the same amount—the very amount he had promised to pay them. As you can imagine, that wasn't going to cut it for the workers who had put in an entire day's work. They cried foul, demanding more than the workers who had only worked a few hours. But the master couldn't have been clearer. He was the master, and he had agreed to pay everyone the same amount. No one forced anyone to work, and the pay was still very good.

It is this matter of comparing our work with others that was also tearing up the older brother as he chewed out his father. He was being paid handsomely already, much more than the servants and much more than he deserved. In fact, lest we forget, the father had already distributed two-thirds of his inheritance to the older son, which meant he was rich beyond his wildest dreams simply because he had been born. This is why the father said to him in verse 31, "All that is mine is yours." He hadn't earned this inheritance. In fact, it had been given to him early because of the foolishness of his little brother. He had benefited from the younger brother's prodigal decision.

But in the mind of the older brother, it wasn't enough. He felt that even a single goat given to his little brother by his father was somehow robbing him of something he deserved. This brother no doubt owned goats as far as the eye could see—after all, he was chief heir to a very wealthy man. When you think of it in these terms, we see that the older brother attitude is not a fairness problem or even a provision problem, but rather a heart problem.

Many church leaders lead with this attitude, and more than

that, they don't lead their members away from this attitude. The result is that church can feel less like the extravagant party that the Father desires and more like a solemn get-together of insiders eating the same old food. Again, having a welcome sign on your church lawn or a coffee bar in your foyer does not produce the culture of the Father's kingdom. This is much deeper stuff—the stuff of your heart and the hearts of the people around you who call your particular church their own.

The bottom line is that God throws parties for his kids who come home, no matter how dirty, wasteful, or sinful they have been. Older brothers, however, throw fits—and if you find yourself word vomiting like the older brother, Jesus says your words are reflecting your heart, so you should pay attention to them. As church leaders and members, we must become intentional in authentically leading our churches away from the older brother attitude.

DIVING DEEPER AND DARKER

We have so much more to be learned from the older brother's speech. First, it's obvious he had not been watching the horizon for his little brother to return. He was busy doing other things, and he didn't care if the father was spending so much time staring at the mountains—he certainly wasn't going to do it.

So he missed out on the best part of the story. He wasn't there when the father ran to meet his younger son. He didn't know his brother was humble and repentant, offering to do the very thing he himself probably would have begrudgingly suggested for his no-good brother—work as a hired hand. He didn't know that his brother had confessed his sin before God too.

The older brother attitude causes us to miss the best part of the whole Jesus experience, the part where he runs to those in trouble and begins showering them with grace, restoration, and a place to belong. We become too busy doing something else on the farm and calling it "the father's business," but the truth is, we're missing the Father's business of welcoming home his children.

But we don't have to miss the best part. Who knows? If the older brother had been privy to the intimate, moving exchange between his dad and brother, perhaps it would have softened his heart. Perhaps just seeing his brother in his lowly condition would have made a difference too. After all, at this point in the story, the younger son had been given a bath, new clothes, a shave, jewelry, and who knows what else. Maybe the older brother saw him from a distance all prettied up, and he just assumed he showed up that way, which once again tweaked his twisted sense of fairness, based not on the generosity of his father but on the scarcity of his own greedy heart. Again, this is pure speculation and not intended to detract from the details of the parable as Jesus told it, but it is not a far cry from the character the older brother exhibited.

My bet, however, is that the older brother had not laid eyes on his younger brother. We certainly do know from Jesus' own words that the older brother did not go into the party to greet anyone, including the younger brother. He kept his distance on purpose, which also distanced him from the intentions of the father's heart.

Jesus knew a thing or two about coming close to those who rejected him and his Father's ways. He was often berated by the religious elite for eating with prostitutes, tax collectors, and other undesirables. However, coming close was a key component of his mission—and the incarnation itself. He looked people in the eyes that the Pharisees would cross to the other side of the street to avoid.

It's easier to hate someone you're not actually looking at from across a table. This is why social media is such a hotbed for vicious verbal assaults that are inhumane and cruel. It seems that so many "normal" people could not be capable of such hate speech toward so many other people, even if just for the sake of simple decency and civility. But as we have learned, when you don't look someone in the eyes—seeing their pain, their expression, and more—it is so much easier to lash out at them because they are not truly people in that moment; they are just categories. Jesus laid aside elements of his own divinity so he could know and experience the human condition, complete with temptation, and thus also sympathize with the weaknesses of real people (Hebrews 4:15), all of whom were sinners.

Isn't this how we treat people outside of the faith, or even outside of our social, denominational, or political alignments? We act as if they are subhuman; we may even believe it. Regardless, they are certainly not connected to us in any form or fashion. In this older brother mindset, people stop being people to us and instead become labels: Democrat, Republican, Black, White, Latino, Asian, Liberal, Conservative, Wealthy, Poor, Nationalist, Immigrant, Pro-Lifer, Pro-Choicer, Redneck, City Slicker, Catholic, Protestant, Reformed, Baptist, Pentecostal, Jew, Muslim, Straight, Gay, and a million other titles that allow us to curtly crumple up their value in a one-word ball so we can toss it aside like a discarded candy wrapper. And we don't even feel guilty for littering, because, after all, they are *just* a (insert label here)—small and insignificant to our lives.

We rarely realize what we're doing because we think we are throwing away the *issue* with which we disagree, not the *people* themselves, especially when their issue seems especially heinous to us. In some cases, the issue truly is one of clear right and wrong. We may be right in assuming that others are living their lives according to destructive, sinful, ungodly principles and patterns. The older brother made a lot of solid points in his speech to his father. The younger son had indeed disrespected the father and the family, having wasted his resources and almost his life on things displeasing to the father.

The difference between the older brother and the father, however, was that the father refused to deny the God-breathed value of the younger son, even though the son rejected and wasted this value through his choices. We must never forget that all people are inherently fashioned with value and worth because they bear God's image. Even when we mess up in the way we carry his image, we can never escape possessing it.

The father separated the boy's behavior from his worth, which created the potential for him to come home and begin living as the beloved son he had always been. This is key: he had been loved from before the time when he had made so many poor choices, which meant the father now had the choice of whether to continue loving him after his poor choices. The father's attitude and actions epitomized the foundational grace of the real gospel—the one many of us think we believe, just as the older brother thought he believed in the value system of his father. He couldn't see that his actions and attitudes made him an unlikely enemy of his father's plan. He missed the amazing grace the father extended to him also, as the father reasoned with him to love his brother rather than throwing him off the farm.

Enemy may seem like a strong word, but if loving the younger son was the father's chief mission, then the words of the older brother align him against that mission. If you remember earlier in the story, the servant had told him, "Your brother has come." But in his subsequent conversation with the father, the older brother rejected any familial connection to the other son when he said, "But when this *son of yours* came . . ." In other words, he no longer considered him to be his brother.

What a dagger! And what compelling evidence of the way we can easily begin treating those who have strayed from the faith, deny the faith, deny the way we live out the faith, or have hurt us with their version of the faith! To us, they make a mockery of the faith, but we don't realize that denying them the divinely inherited value the father has bestowed on them and still feels for them is a mockery of the faith as well.

The older son was completely done with his brother, as if his actions had somehow negated their blood familial connection. In this case, the application to our lives would be disregarding someone's humanity because of their mistake—thus feeling no obligation to continue loving them and no guilt for holding them in contempt—or disregarding their place in the family of God, perhaps even when they no longer consider themselves believers or followers of Jesus. By doing this, just like the older brother, we can more easily justify our complete lack of concern or even our outright hostility toward them.

As someone who has actually been thrown out of church, I get it. If you've ever been hurt by someone in the church, I imagine you get it too. Thinking of "those people" in subhuman terms helps us distance ourselves from the pain, anger, and disappointment we feel toward them. It is a natural, human coping mechanism; it just happens to not be the culture of the father's farm.

I'm not suggesting we should remain in unhealthy, unaligned, or abusive relationships in church or in life because doing so is the godly action. Many times, separation from a toxic relationship or toxic theology is the best move. This isn't about the physical separation between the two brothers—that was already established. It was about the spiritual separation between the heart of the older brother and the heart of the father. The father was only asking that the older brother share in rejoicing what should occur when a repentant son returns home. He wasn't asking the older son to give up any of his own inheritance or freedom; he was only asking him to care about the life—a life of one who has come back from the dead—of his younger brother.

The older brother wasn't having it though. He thought he had valid reasons to reject the father's pleas. We can learn a key lesson here for understanding the way we can function—sometimes unknowingly—in an older brother spirit. The brother recited some of the specific ways the younger son had acted, which was obviously meant to validate the fit he was throwing, as well as the throwing out of the younger brother's worth to the family. He said, "This son of yours . . . has devoured your property with prostitutes."

This part may not raise any red flags, but I invite you to pay attention. When we tell the story of the "prodigal," we usually focus on the younger son spending his money lavishly on prostitutes and other shameful endeavors, but if we examine the text, this is the first mention of prostitution, the most scandalous accusation. As I've already pointed out, Jesus had simply said the young man had squandered his inheritance in wasteful living. That was it. Jesus never said the younger brother did anything sinful.

It was the older brother who either conjured up this new information and inserted it into the story, or perhaps he was secretly surveilling his brother the whole time he was gone in order to keep accusations on the ready, just in case he ever showed back up. The former makes more sense than the latter, but I'm never surprised by the lengths people with the older brother attitude will go to discredit people in their time of repentance. Older brothers with this attitude can sometimes accuse younger brothers of things they haven't done or shouldn't be held accountable for.

When Jesus was telling the story, he never said anything about prostitution. When the younger son rehearsed his speech of repentance, he never said anything about prostitution. When the father spoke to both sons, he never said anything about prostitution. And yet the main accusation against the younger brother—the one that, consequently, most of us have always believed to be true—is levied by one who shouldn't have such information.

I can think of several ways to envision what could have happened here—and I don't think that imagining some of them is feckless speculation. The reason is that the attitude of the older brother was tied to definitive events and patterns, ones on which Jesus didn't fully expound. When we are caught in such an attitude, we can easily miss the actions and attitudes that create and bolster it. Yes, one of the servants could have mentioned the prostitution. There are many options, but this information was not communicated by the younger brother or the father, at least according to Jesus' telling of it.

The point I'm trying to make is that the older brother attitude is one of accusation and ultimately deception. Who knows, he may have been accurate about what the younger brother had done while living abroad, but he was deceiving himself about what was right in the eyes of his father—and about his own worthiness based on the fact that he had never engaged in the specific sins of his brother. (His own sins somehow didn't bother him.)

Jesus knew his audience, and he knew that the Pharisees had many ways of accusing people away from God's blessing. My take from the simplest reading of the text is that the older brother was lying—simply filling in the blanks he felt the father was overlooking.

Religious people with older brother attitudes do this often. They keep tabs on all the bad people in the world just so they can accuse them, all the while claiming they are just trying to remain informed as they mind their own business back at the Father's house. This generally leads to a series of statements:

Well, he's Catholic, and you know what all Catholics believe, right?
Well, she had an affair, and you know what they say about all
people like that: once a cheater, always a cheater!
Well, she's a Republican, and all Republicans hate immigrants.
Well, he's a Democrat, and all Democrats believe it's okay to kill
babies. I read an article about it in the New York Times . . .
or was it on Twitter?

The truth is, the older brother wasn't being truthful. He would have done anything for self-preservation, including being dishonest and accusing his brother of something of which he had no actual proof.

Of course, there's always the chance that the younger brother had used his money to hire prostitutes—it certainly isn't out of the question. Let's say it was true. In that case, the older brother just couldn't understand or accept the grace of the father. In his mind, *that* sin was the sin of no return. This is where the rubber meets the road in many churches: when we live as if one type of sin—different from our own, mind you—is worse than others and negates the effects of the blood of Christ to cleanse, forgive, heal, and restore all people to a relationship with the Father and his people. Every group has a target leper.

JUST IMAGINE

None of us want to think of ourselves as older brothers. In fact, my bet is that if you were to read the descriptions of the older brother—entitled, disrespectful, petty, and dishonest—to anyone in church, no one would raise a hand and say, "Yep, that's me. I'm an older brother!"

But the fact remains that our churches are filled with older brothers, which is why younger brothers sometimes don't return home to their father. I just think of the older brother attitude that kicked my family out of church. Can you imagine what would have happened if the younger brother had been greeted by the older brother first instead of the father? It would have been a verbal bloodbath of prideful accusation and rejection—and the younger brother would have agreed with it. After all, he was already condemning himself when he arrived. The older brother attitude would have supported the narrative already at work in the returning son's heart and mind—the same narrative at work in most people who want to approach God and find rest but know they don't deserve it.

This scenario is what's happening all across our country every Sunday. People are doing their part and approaching the Father's house, but instead of being greeted by loving fathers, they are being stopped at Checkpoint Older Brother on the far outskirts of faith—the badlands of religion where only those who look and act a certain way can have access to safety and provision in the Father's house. And even if the older brother would have let the younger brother pass, my bet is he would have agreed to the three-point sermon of his misguided sibling, showing him the servant's quarters, the servant's table in the back of the kitchen, and the servant's role out in the fields while Older Brother supervised. He would have been just fine letting an undeserving sinner spend the rest of his life as a second-class team member (in our cases, a second-class Christian).

But Jesus' closing remarks in this story should illuminate the final word on the Father's heart here—the one he expects all of his children to accept with joy and express with authenticity:

> And he said to him, "Son, you are always with me, and
> all that is mine is yours. It was *fitting* to celebrate and be

glad, for this your brother was dead, and is alive; he was lost, and is found."

Luke 15:31–32, emphasis mine

First of all, the message for anyone who calls themselves a disciple of Christ is this: you are already rich beyond your wildest dreams. As the father said, "You are always with me, and all that is mine is yours." Talk about a lack of fairness—the father was speaking this to a truly unruly son. I empathize with this as a son who has often failed to reflect my Father's ways. Even so, the father is kind and inviting to *both* brothers.

This the way of the Father, the heart he sent Christ to reveal to the world and that is still so hard for all of us in this world to accept. We can't envision a God who overlooks our shortcomings out of love, even though we know he is one who has revealed to us that "love covers a multitude of sins."[2] We still want fairness, which means that while we may be able to sing and recite the basic theological building blocks of the gospel, we still don't truly understand or believe that Jesus came for the purpose of doing what only he could do—extinguishing the unquenchable forest fire of sin, which rages about to destroy everything, by casting himself onto the flames. He is the love that has covered sin.

Justice has been accomplished through the punishment Jesus accepted on our behalf. He took what we deserved, so now we can be free to forgive others the debt they owe out of a constant, joyful realization of the forgiveness given to us as well.

The father showed the older brother the same grace he had shown the younger. That's kind of God's thing: "He gives more grace."[3] The culture of his kingdom must begin there, because the gospel begins there. If we skip that part, then who cares how talented our worship bands are; how well-organized and well-funded our programs are; or how articulate, charming, or knowledgeable our pastors are from the stage? No one cares, and that brings us to the crossroad of the crisis we face in the church today. Again, most of the problems people have with God and church are due to inaccurate, faulty, graceless images of the Father reinforced by the attitudes of older brothers they meet at the door—that is, on social media, on billboards, and above all else, inside church buildings themselves.

But I pray that my words reflect the words of the father in the story, because, believe it or not, God's answer is still to give more grace. He knows that through the truth revealed in his radical grace—his literal kindness—we are led to true repentance.[4] All of our own sins—past, present, and future—have been completely paid for by the sacrifice of Jesus at the cross, and it is important to remind ourselves of these truths so we don't drift into older brother mindsets, somehow thinking that someone else needs the Father's grace more than we do.

We do not stand justified before the Father because we have been faithful; we stand justified before the Father because Jesus Christ has done *all the work*. In fact, though we may work in and about the Father's business, in terms of our status before God, we contribute *nothing* to our salvation, much in the same way that a dead person who is raised to life does not—and indeed cannot—raise his hand first and request it. Dead people do nothing but remain dead unless they are acted on by a supernatural, outside force who is not limited by the confines of death: "But God shows his love for us in that while we were still sinners [*that is, dead in our sins*], Christ *died for us*."[5]

Just imagine if the older brother would have realized the level of grace that the father had already lavished on him—remember, he was already a millionaire (at least) simply because he was a son. Just imagine if he would have understood the basic premise of life on the farm—the father's riches given to sons and servants in mercy. Just imagine if he would have run out to his brother with his father to hear the outpouring of his sibling's repentant heart and his father's overwhelming display of affection. He could have been a part of preparing the party of the decade. And unlike the bitter, entitled, bratty son he had become, he would have been grateful, fulfilled, and, above all, pleasing to the father who was the source of life for everyone on the farm.

What if we were to do the same in our churches? The result would be a safe landing place for prodigals (inside and outside the church). It would feel different, not because of gimmicks, gifts, or gadgets, but because it would actually be different. People wouldn't come to hear a certain speaker or a certain worship leader. They would run to the church—and not just on Sundays—because the people themselves would be known as a pleasant estate where the Father throws elaborate "welcome home" parties for long-lost children alongside the efforts of *all* of his other children who are authentically ecstatic to see their siblings return home, where they truly belong.

A PARTY CULTURE

Creating the kind of culture in your church that watches the horizon and makes room for and celebrates younger brothers coming home is something you must decide to do every day. It won't be a onetime decision. I can remember one event in particular that deeply affected the culture of our church, as well as my role in it as a leader.

When I began at LifePoint Church, I remember specifically asking the Lord to help me pastor a church that my nonbelieving friends would want to attend. I wanted to lead a church that was passionate for God's Word, for prayer, for change, and for ministry to young families. I wanted us to be a church that never made the lost or unbelieving person feel unwelcomed.

When I began, all who attended were believers and passionate for God to do something great. I have a Pentecostal background, and in that stream, people tend to have an openness to more expressive moments and responses in the worship services.

In my second week, as I was standing on the floor during the music time, I was worshiping and excited to preach. Just then, someone from the middle of the room walked onto the stage, stood next to the keyboard player, held out her hand to instruct him to soften his playing, and took over the entire service as she began to share a declaration she believed was a "word from God" for the church. She shut down the worship leader and the entire band, speaking loudly and matter-of-factly over us all. She shared some affirming sentiments, threw in some skewed versions of random Bible passages, and ended the whole experience with, "Thus saith the Lord." (Incidentally, that was the only part of the whole speech that was in King James English . . . and it didn't really fit at all with what I had planned to preach.)

Right now, some of you who are from the Pentecostal or charismatic tribes are reading this story with great familiarity, wondering if I "let it flow" or if I was another youngster who would "quench the Spirit of God." Some of you may be reading this from a mainline or Reformed tradition, wondering what kind of church I'm leading, and you're curious if this really happens. Stay with me.

As soon as her declaration began, I reached behind my back to cover the power button on my microphone in case I needed to interrupt or correct anything being said. Fortunately, it was all very positive. I kept my mic off and leaned to my associate pastor standing next to me, and I asked, "Does this happen all the time?" He told me it did, so I wondered how I was going to handle this. I was the new guy, and I understood why this was happening, but I started thinking with the filter of someone who was new or who had never met Jesus. Would we prefer our gifts, or would we prefer their presence?

The next day, I called the woman who had interrupted the service. I had met her once, and she was a very sweet person. I shared with her my appreciation for her love of our church and thanked her for showing her confidence in me to be her pastor by voting for me just a month earlier. I shared some vision with her about the structure and order of our services moving forward. Then I told her we wanted to be a church where outsiders can come and meet the Lord without confusion. I talked about Paul's direction in 1 Corinthians 14 that all things must be done decently and in order. I pointed out his view that prophetic leaders lead in prophetic moments, and that there is a submitting to the spiritual leadership in the church context. I quoted Paul's words: "The spirits of prophets are subject to prophets."[6]

Then I simply asked, "In order to maintain a culture that is caring for outsiders and lost people coming in and make sure all things are flowing in the same direction, and to maintain a unity in our Sunday gatherings, if you ever feel stirred to share something with our church, would you please not interrupt our services and instead share those thoughts with me first so I'll be able to confirm whether it's appropriate to share in the context of the service for the sake of those present?"

The discussion that followed was unfortunate. I was confronted for not trusting God, believing in the gift of prophesy, and making room for her to do what she wanted to do as a member. She suggested I might not be the pastor she thought I was or could support, and she told me she'd probably leave as a result (which she did). I didn't argue, but I listened because I was committed to speak up for those who would be showing up and to think not of our own interests but the interests of others. I'm fully convinced that the gifts of the Holy Spirit are available for Christians today. But I also know that lost people matter to the heart of God, and the gifts should flow in a way that reveals his heart more than how gifted we are.

After I finished, I felt that warm-blood-boiling feeling of anxiety inside—after all, we didn't need to lose any faithful attenders or givers. But I had this sense from the Lord that this woman already had everything we were working for in terms of salvation and heaven. Still, like the older brother, she may have been missing the big picture of the Father's heart—that we're not doing church for the sake of us; we are keeping an eye out for the one who is missing.

As we come to the close of this chapter, as well as our time in this particular parable, let's address the way this story ends. We find the older brother and the father in a stalemate, stuck in a conversation about the way the older brother doesn't want to welcome home the younger brother. My heart breaks, because this is exactly the state of much of modern churchianity today. Obviously, many churches are getting this right, but I'm concerned that many of us in the church world are getting it wrong. We are stunted in reaching the lost, baptizing new believers, sending new missionaries, starting new churches—not because we can't draw people with good sermons, quality programming, and excellent events, but because, amid the trappings of church, we still don't share the Father's attitude toward outsiders.

Just as we have no record that the older son ever came around, we have no guarantee that the American church is going to come around either. Many Christians can't understand how they can welcome "sinners" into their communities, which shows how backward our faith value system has become. Jesus always intended for his house—that is, his people—to be a place where sinners are welcomed. Like a hospital expecting sick people, a restaurant expecting hungry people, and a barbershop expecting guys with shaggy hair to come, churches should absolutely expect sinners to show up—all the time!

Most people like it when I talk about our church being a place where anyone is welcome to come and be wrecked by Jesus; in fact, if I focused more heavily on just that, I bet it would relieve the pressure you're feeling when you think about church being a place for dirty prodigals. As I've already pointed out, Jesus does absolutely change our lives—but it comes as a result of the Father's overwhelming desire for every child to come home. The younger son came as he was, not as he thought he had to be to be accepted. He simply could not afford to clean up his life first. That would be the responsibility of the Father.

As we think about the culture of our churches, I challenge you to think deeply about the revolutionary rhetoric of Jesus' language in this parable. He said the older brother didn't just hear *what had happened*; he heard *what was happening* right then. The father's joyful reaction to his son's return sounded like a real party, the kind you would want to attend. It was loud, as evidenced by the fact that the older brother heard the sounds of "music and dancing."

The father's final words in the chapter best reveal God's heart on the matter: "It was fitting to celebrate and be glad, for this your brother was dead, and is alive; he was lost, and is found." The whole world is full of churches of all different sizes, expressions, looks, and traditions, but these words must inform our thoughts about the culture that God intends every one of his churches to possess and express. If we wonder how it should feel, the Father answers us very plainly: it is fitting to celebrate and be glad when those who have been far away want to come near.

God describes this process not in terms of church as we know it—preferences, speakers, vibe, and the like—but rather in terms of life and death. It is that important to him, which means it should be that important to us. Church should be a place where the party for the person turning or returning to God can be heard from miles around. It should be evident that we care about lost things, just as the Father does.

To be clear one last time, I'm not talking about the volume of music in a church, the decorations in the building, or the epic nature of a church's services or special events. If all of those things are in place, which can be awesome, it will still eventually prove to be only a mirage that promises water for the desperately thirsty heart but falls short on delivering any authentic refreshment. In fact, I think it's detrimental to promote an atmosphere of acceptance for outsiders but not have this ethic in your local church culture—that is, in the belief system of their hearts as it relates to the heart of the gospel itself. It can do more damage than if the lost never would have tried to come home to your church in the first place.

The greatest expression of this "party" is not so much *what* we do as the *way* we do whatever we do—that is, the way we legitimately desire that people far away from the Father will find a place to be cleaned up, fed, restored, and celebrated. Our attitudes are either the party that is heard from miles away or the place where we are pitching the sulking fit. If Jesus didn't have to convince Christians to act like him, just imagine how fun his church would truly be!

I could share a host of practical ideas for being party-ready for those who are coming home, but a lot of other books out there can do this. I will at least say that we begin before the lost ever even fully make it onto the property. Again, this is merely a methodology that we hope reflects a true culture. Methodology cannot trump culture, which means you can't attack the older brother attitude from the outside in. It requires a constant dialogue about the heart, which is exactly what the father initiated with the older brother.

The bottom line is this: establishing a "heart of the father" culture should be where the most essential energies of a local church are expended. Otherwise, the church will build something that may look impressive but will ultimately be undermined by a faulty foundation because it doesn't reflect the Father's heart. If our best efforts don't look like the Father's best efforts, we shouldn't expect the transformation of lives that only the Father can accomplish.

The tragic results of not having this foundation generally happen in two ways. First, a church remains constantly in flux as people float in with eagerness and, in a few months or maybe years, float right back out in disappointment or bitterness because what was promised in the beginning—a full and transformed life—was not delivered. And without the Father's heart at the center of the culture, it certainly can never be delivered.

Second, a church with especially excellent speakers, leaders, or resources just keeps growing to become full of members whose lives really don't look like disciples. Like a balloon, the surface area easily expands, but there is very little substance within. Any culture other than the Father's is a balloon just waiting to pop. They are one small pinprick of offense or scandal from a huge boom—a sound much less pleasant to the outside world than a party.

Kingdom culture is a decision made over and over again—a reminding of ourselves and one's community about the true condition of our hearts without the grace of Christ. As we immerse ourselves in real relationships where confession, repentance, and community are truly realized and practiced daily, we will be, and will continue to become, disciples. We will stop throwing fits and instead start throwing parties alongside the Father.

PART 2

THE PARABLE
OF THE
SOWER

CHAPTER 5

SEEDS, SOIL, AND SUCH

The Seeds Always Work;
The Soil Does Not

Your job is not to change people's lives, but they should change. Your job is not to make churches grow, but they should grow. Growth is a funny thing—well, mostly funny. If you're anything like me, "natural" growth is rarely a good thing. For example, if I don't watch what I'm eating and don't exercise regularly, I will experience very rapid "natural" growth—and naturally, I will have to buy a new pair of jeans.

At the time of this writing, my wife, Stephanie, and I recently moved into a new house with our four daughters. We love everything about it, but we especially like that there are woods behind it. Everyone craves a little bit of the great outdoors merely a stone's throw from the great indoors. A beautifully wild, yet still mostly domesticated destination for untold adventures galore.

However, the space *between* our house and this wooded wonderland—some may call it a "yard"—presents a unique set of challenges to me and to homeowners around the world. For the sake of context, I will confess that I'm not great at producing an amazing yard, but I love the beauty of a manicured and lush lawn. My next-door neighbor is amazing at this, and his yard is hands down the gold standard for the whole neighborhood. Perfectly edged, thick and green, and zero weeds. I am trying hard to get my yard to match this standard, and he is such an encouraging and patient lawn Jedi. It takes time, and it takes work.

The thing is, if I work hard at tending my lawn, it will produce what I'm after. If I don't do anything with my yard, then natural growth takes over. In no time at all, not even a full season, my yard will decline, and thorns and thistles will just naturally spring up everywhere, with no effort from me. Those weeds will need treatment and mowing, but they aren't what I'd prefer to manage.

Simply put, it's growth, but not *healthy* growth.

Even so, it can look the part. If I leave my yard to its own devices and then mow it to a uniform consistency every few weeks, it can look green and lush. But it is only an illusion. It is not real grass, but rather an impressively manicured carpet of weeds. It takes a lot of work to keep a yard full of weeds looking like a yard full of grass—and it is very frustrating work. I have to constantly pull up and chop back the weeded overgrowth, sometimes exposing raw dirt that is nothing more than gross, thorny, stony ground.

But if I truly want a "lawn," a term only fancy people use, I have to consistently keep cutting away the unhealthy parts and consistently keep resowing the right kinds of seeds. It's a constant process, and it's not for the faint of heart—or the faint of back, for that matter. Plus, I can't let my neighbor down and be "that guy"!

I have experienced growth in other areas of life as well. LifePoint Church has been on an incredible trajectory of growth since those early days in the Taupe Mahal—an unofficial title a few of us used to describe our original church building due to its less-than-brilliant color choices, a story I will soon unpack in more detail. The growth of our church in Clarksville may be one of the main reasons you're reading this book—and one of the main reasons there is a book to read in the first place. In 2018, *Outreach* magazine named LifePoint Church the "fastest growing church in America."[1] I must admit I was profoundly surprised and humbled when I got the call from them. This is not a label I was ever really interested in, nor one I ever thought we would be given. The truth is, I have mixed emotions about that reality. What God has done here is absolutely amazing, and we give him all the credit and celebrate every single bit of it. But at times, as the pastor of this "fastest growing church," I feel like a little kid carrying a very expensive vase, doing my best to move it without dropping it and watching it break into a million little shards—primarily because it does not belong to me.

No one is more astonished or overjoyed than me about the growth we've experienced. It has been a wild ride, much wilder than most people really know. In my experience, people in the "church world" tend to hear stories about "the fastest growing churches in America" and naturally assume a lot of things about them. For the most part, they assume we're riding around our huge church building on magical unicorns (that is, when we're not rolling around in piles of money like Scrooge McDuck—shout out to my daughters). In their minds, the sun never sets and the party never ends at a "megachurch."

I get it, especially when a pastor or a church has spent years toiling in a certain community, struggling to win people to the hope of the gospel that leads them to be firmly rooted and grounded in a community of faith where they can actually be and make disciples. Sometimes it just feels like growth is an impossible pursuit. I've been there myself many times—and every time I go to a church that is bigger than mine, I'm reminded of those same feelings. They are still difficult. For that leader—and for me—I know the struggle is very real.

It can begin to feel like failure—and it can be easy to think that the yard is always greener on the other side of town where attendance is high and morale is even higher. To this end, I've had plenty of pastors say things to me like, "Well, if I had your numbers of people and resources, our church would be growing too." I always try to exercise extra care here for my brothers and sisters in ministry who are facing struggles that weigh down their hearts and minds with discouragement. I never want to come off as the latest church growth "guru." I am not. We are not. In fact, I'm often stunned that this has happened here.

The Bible is clear that some people plant the seeds of the gospel and some people water the seeds of the gospel. And I am convinced it is God who grows his church. We are merely stewards of the growth God is bringing to his church. That is truly my position—to steward what God is doing. We don't get to choose what God does; we only get to choose how we react to what God chooses to do. It may seem like false humility here, but I am convinced that this is God's church and that I am a steward and a worker here. It's all his, not mine. I manage God's stuff. He chose to grow it; I didn't. But to that end, the way we manage God's growth starts with the way we manage what God has given us.

That's what this section is all about: the way things—more accurately, the way people and churches—grow. This should be a natural, logical progression from the topic of the first section—that is, understanding the foundational culture of the Father and his desire that all people find his farm and his family to be an authentically enthusiastic house to which they can either turn or return. From there, we can turn our attention to the ways people become healthy members of this household of faith—or at least, that's the way it *should* work.

MINDING OUR
OWN BUSINESS

Unfortunately, the sequence described above often isn't a natural progression. Pastors and leaders don't usually lead with questions about the culture of their church established from the heart of the Father. Instead, they tend to lead with questions about the topic of this section of the book—growth—assuming, or perhaps hoping, it will somehow lead to the principles of the first section of the book, namely, health and culture. There is often an assumption that their culture is already healthy and that the heart of the Father is already evident in everything they say and do as leaders, as well as in communicating to the community outside their walls.

The result is that most of the church world chases after this elusive Sasquatch called church growth, which for them mainly means rising attendance and financial stability. It wouldn't be too histrionic to compare the chasing of church growth to the California Gold Rush of the mid-nineteenth century. Pastors and leaders plant churches all over the country, just hoping to strike it rich. After all, they hear stories of churches that have seemingly ascended to elite levels of attendance in a short amount of time, so it's obvious it can happen anywhere—and to anyone. Let me be clear, I'm not throwing growth under the proverbial church bus here. I just want to challenge the motivations of our insatiable hunger for growth and encourage a better way toward health and a healthy culture, which will help produce an environment for growth.

No one description or rule completely covers all people, including church planters. I'm a huge fan of church planting, and we have been committed to helping church planters through contributions and partnerships with some of the leading church planting organizations. We will always be ready to support the church planting process as a means of advancing the kingdom of heaven. I have observed that most people who do this ministry have nothing but the best intentions at heart. Most church planters do a lot of research and set out with a genuine desire to reach people in the areas where they are.

Let me share a few observations I've noticed as we've resourced church planters. Many leaders plant churches in growing areas where wealthy families are building houses and corporations are building new plants—areas where the demographics are pleasing and advantageous for sustaining attendance and offerings. Sometimes they even do so in the knowledge that there are already dozens upon dozens of new church plants in the same area, but they feel fine opening up their own little operation next door to the others—after all, it is a free-for-all. This may feel like a jab, but it's actually a reflection of many of my own sinister ambitions in the early years of ministry.

As church planters, we mostly end up competing for the affections and treasures of the same families who spend a few years rotating among our churches trying to decide who offers the best amenities for their specific family needs. We may have programs—or plans to start programs—to serve the poor and marginalized, but our main plan is to grow our churches by first winning over the influential.

If we just get the first group in place, imagine how much good we can do for the second group, right? This is often the mentality that marks the mission. If you ask most leaders and pastors about their motivations for working and serving in the church, they would point to the call of God on their lives to impact the world for Christ. No one can ever question this—it would legitimately be insulting to do so.

But what if we open up our hearts to the *biblical* idea of

growth in God's church, and what if doing so requires us to look honestly at the way we think of it right now? Just as medical exams are helpful and observing healthy medical advice is advantageous, aligning our expectations and processes with the culture of God's kingdom as revealed in Scripture is a preventive gift that leads to actual, sustained health.

If we carry the medical metaphor further, many people who have gone under the knife had absolutely no idea at some point in their recent past that anything was even wrong. They just chalked up their back pain, groin pain, or shortness of breath to the weather, getting older, or an old sports injury. In other words, they were not in the best of health, but they didn't know it. Such is the condition of many in the modern Western church. Without an honest exam or even a surgery, we may assume we are relatively healthy—which we tend to judge by the numbers.

In the church, it's not blood pressure or triglycerides; it's weekend attendance and offering amounts. So we may think we are healthy, especially if a certain number of people are still showing up and contributing. All is well. The opposite assumption also plagues many leaders with senseless insecurities—that if a certain number of people are *not* showing up or are pulling back on their financial support, then we are completely failing.

The point is worth belaboring, because it is *the* point. If the abiding principles of the parable of the two sons are not truly taken to heart and applied to the concepts of church, then the principles of the next parable will do us little good. We may assume we think a certain way, but God's Word leads us to discern the ways we are *really* thinking—and if church growth is our actual highest goal, above the heart of the Father to create a safe place for prodigals to return, then even if we do experience "growth," we will simply join the statistics of the millions who are selling everything in order to chase some utopian dream of striking it rich, and most of them end up in spiritual poverty. Surely this shouldn't be so.

The heart of the Father must remain our main business.

With that foundation firmly established, let's make the transition between the two stories. Jesus ended the parable of the two sons with the awkward conversation between the older brother and the father that took place outside the party. For the sake of conversation, would it not be a fascinating social experiment to consider what life was like on the farm once the initial party ended and everyone got back to the business of living life together day in and day out? They would probably have "grown" into being a healthy family, discovering what life together looked like with all of its complications of their shared past and complexities of their shared present.

For the church, this is a perfect expression of the concept of discipleship, which is the kind of growth most people reading books on "church growth" really don't want to hear because, once again, everyone assumes that what they're already doing in church is discipleship. So then, there is *growth*—the way people continually become and continually make disciples—and then there is *growth*—the way a local church expands in people, resources, and influence. Again, I want to be clear. I believe in both kinds of growth, just in the right order.

It would be great to have both kinds, and in general, the second follows the first. However, there may well be instances when the second precedes the first, and this kind of growth can be quite unhealthy—a yard full of weeds does not a lawn make. But all around, growth seems to be the main topic of interest for those of us who lead, attend, and desire to positively affect the churches we serve.

Since we are being painfully honest in grace, let me slice a little deeper with something every pastor, leader, and member should know: you *cannot* make a church grow. Let that sink in, and resist the temptation to nod your head in agreement so you can read ahead to "growth secrets." There are none—the heart of the Father *is* the secret he is desperately trying to reveal to the world but we keep muzzling with faulty ideas of religion and church growth.

You can't make God's church grow for a couple of reasons. The main one is that it is *not your church.* Pastors have a bad habit of calling churches their own. "Hey, have you heard about what's going on over at Mike's church?" It's standard fare in our conversations, and I don't think we mean anything by it, which is the problem, because if we're discussing the living, breathing entity nearest and dearest to the very heart of the Father, when we speak of her, we should probably mean something by it. It is *not* our church; it is his—the same holds true for the local church you attend or lead. We can't make it grow; we can only steward God's growth, although we can certainly impede it from growing rightly.

The growth of God's church is God's business, which is why we often *get in his way* instead of *live in his ways.* Church is made up of people, so the same is true of individuals. You just can't make a person grow—not even yourself. The bottom line is God says he is the one who brings an increase. One person plants a seed. Another person waters it. But it is God who brings growth.[2] When you grow tomatoes, you can buy the best plant, get the best topsoil, use a whole box of Miracle-Gro; you can name and claim growth, shout the victory over every pest in the garden, and pray with fasting for the tomatoes to grow in Jesus' name. But that tomato plant will still grow at the pace for which the Lord has designed it.

Growth is God's business, not ours.

At LifePoint Church, the community I'm honored to serve,

we don't take any credit for growing our church. We do, however, take responsibility for stewarding it and managing it. This is the reality of what we are called to do. We'll explore this in much greater depth in the parable of the talents.

But for now, suffice it to say that people ask us a lot of questions, *not* about our stewardship, but about our hidden, unique, almost mystical formula for explosive growth. As if we own a box of ecclesiastical silver bullets, we are often asked, "What are the keys to your fast rate of growth?" or "What are the top five things you did to see such amazing growth?" or "If you could point to one thing that really caused LifePoint Church to grow, what is it?" We have no silver bullets. We do the same basic things every church does. We preach from the Bible too. For the most part, these questions are broken.

If we truly believe the Bible, we didn't do anything to grow our church. In fact, if the growth of our church is the only reason people want to read this book, I toyed with the possibility of using an alternative title: *What the Heck Happened to Our Church?* Publishers didn't seem to care much for that option.

The point is that when it comes to someone's life or to a community of lives, we simply must stop acting—no matter how much we claim to believe otherwise—that growth is a matter completely up to us. Yes, we have a key role as stewards, but we do not have a key role as creators. No respectable farmer plants a seed, waters it, and tends to it, only to stand back, point at the first tiny piece of fruit that appears on the vine, and proclaim, "Look, I have created a tomato!"

Sounds pretty silly, doesn't it? Yet this is exactly what we do so often in our own lives, as well as in our churches. We take ownership of something beyond our abilities to own, which leaves us either completely overwhelmed with a task of regeneration we are incapable of even starting, or experiencing the miracle of growth and suddenly dubbing ourselves as "growth experts." All the while, the biblical process of growth is clear and simple:

- We *plant* something not of our own making.
- We *water* something we can't always see.
- God *creates* something out of the very seeds he gave us to plant in the first place.

Notice that I said the process is *simple*; I did not say it's easy. There's a lot of work involved, but we often tend to be working on the wrong task, exerting energy in the wrong place, and either gaining or losing confidence because we are obsessed with the wrong thing, which is when we focus on results. Those are *God's* results, not our focus.

Let's make room to understand the right things—what we should be doing.

THE NEXT STORY AND THE NATURE OF THE SOIL

Remember where we started. The premise of this book is that Jesus never told us how to "do church." He never explicitly created a color-coded chart that laid out the stages that should accompany a local congregation's establishment, organization, and perpetuation. He never said what to call a local church body or what time the services should begin.

But make no mistake, Jesus was all about the church—and he talked about life as the church repeatedly. Am I contradicting myself here? Not at all. If we understand what God fully intends for those whose lives are hidden in the life of his Son, then Scripture begins to come to life in ways we could never detect before—and especially in Jesus' words in the Gospels. It was Paul who ascribed the metaphor of a "body" to the collective membership of Jesus' church, but it was definitely Jesus who established the idea of the life—his life—that would animate this body, that would not only keep us from eternal death but grant us an eternal life that doesn't wait for future results to begin.

As his people—his church—we're alive right now.

This fact is what motivates me to help churches see this parable point of view. By the "church," I mean the people of Christ—his body. I am talking about those within whom the very life force of the Creator of all life resides, even if only in a dormant, unfruitful state. We're *alive* in Christ, but sometimes we are *asleep* in this world. I praise God for local churches and for the fact that new churches are being planted every year. While many cities are known for having churches on every corner, the church herself sometimes seems to be hiding.

This is at least partly because we don't recognize the connection between the principles Jesus taught in the Gospels and their direct correlation with the way we should be the church—and thus also should do whatever it is the church is supposed to be doing. We seem to have trouble reading between the red lines, because the truth is, Jesus gave us many perspectives on the concept of the way people—and churches—actually grow in health and effectiveness. But too often, we're so familiar with the general idea of something that we stop examining it for deeper perspectives. When we think we have hit the bottom, we stop digging. But I want to dig deeper here.

While many biblical passages use the illustrations of seeds, trees, fruit, and growth, the foundational parable that establishes principles for healthy personal and church growth is the parable of the sower in Matthew 13:3–23—my favorite "church growth" strategy ever given. I'm sure you're familiar with it, since it's been in your Bible as long as you've been reading it. But indulge me as we unpack it with fresh eyes.

> And he told them many things in parables, saying: "A sower went out to sow. And as he sowed, some seeds fell along the path, and the birds came and devoured them. Other seeds fell on rocky ground, where they did not have much soil, and immediately they sprang up, since they had no depth of soil, but when the sun rose they were scorched. And since they had no root, they withered away. Other seeds fell among thorns, and the thorns grew up and choked them. Other seeds fell on good soil and produced grain, some a hundredfold, some sixty, some thirty. He who has ears, let him hear."
>
> *Matthew 13:3–9*

While the first parable we explored utilized the irresistible illustration of family—something every one of us either has or longs for—this parable is a little more specialized for the contemporary reader. To the original listeners in a mostly agrarian society, the concepts of seeds, planting, tending, and reaping would have been second nature—as familiar to them as it would be for us today if I were to create an illustration that uses the example of an iPhone. While farmers are still the backbone of our national economy, most people in our country today are not out sowing seeds as a regular part of their daily lives. Fortunately, you don't have to be a farmer to reap the benefits of Jesus' story.

In fact, though the elements of this story made sense to the hearers, apparently the disciples themselves did not quite catch the gist of what Jesus was trying to communicate: "Then the disciples came and said to him, 'Why do you speak to them in parables?'"[3] In other words, they wanted to know why Jesus didn't just say whatever it is he wanted them to know. Jesus basically indicated that general blindness and deafness keep people from seeing and hearing, but he was willing to reveal the meaning to them.

> "Hear then the parable of the sower: When anyone hears the word of the kingdom and does not understand it, the evil one comes and snatches away what has been sown in his heart. This is what was sown along the path. As for what was sown on rocky ground, this is the one who hears the word and immediately receives it with joy, yet he has no root in himself, but endures for a while, and when tribulation or persecution arises on account of the word, immediately he falls away. As for what was sown among thorns, this is the one who hears the word, but the cares of the world and the deceitfulness of riches choke the word, and it proves unfruitful. As for what was sown on good soil, this is the one who hears the word and understands it. He indeed bears fruit and yields, in one case a hundredfold, in another sixty, and in another thirty."
>
> *Matthew 13:18–23*

Jesus explained his parable to his disciples by defining the seeds, the identities and roles of all the characters, and the nature of the soil. We will move among these concepts throughout this entire section of chapters on this parable, but it suffices to simply say up front that the sower represents the one who speaks the message of the gospel, the seeds represent the word of the kingdom of God, and the soil represents the hearts of people in the crowd.

Understanding these various components of the story is key to applying all of its possible takeaways to our lives as Christians and as leaders—or as both. In fact, out of all of the parables we will explore, this is the one about which Jesus gave the most explanation. It was obvious that the people listening to him speak seemed to not get what he was saying, which is probably indicative of the fact that we just don't get it either. The way Jesus wanted them to think about the process and roles in the communication of his message to people was counterintuitive to their natural way of thinking.

It's probably counterintuitive to our way of thinking as well, so it's a good thing Jesus offered a deeper explanation to his followers. The fact that he did is good news hidden right in the middle of *the* Good News. After all, who among us hasn't completely missed the target with the way we think about or live out the ways of God? It's okay—that doesn't stop Jesus from being willing to sit down with us as his disciples and give us a personal explanation of what he really means for us and for our lives in his church.

The gist of the story is that a sower sowed some seeds through the process of scattering them. This is key because scattering was the most common way of sowing in ancient times. It involved going out into a field and throwing seeds. In other words, the process of sowing really isn't very complicated. It doesn't require genetic seed alteration, the latest in fertilizer development, or million-dollar combines. No, it's just a matter of taking handfuls of seeds and letting them fly. I'm not saying there isn't a high cost or value on the fertilizer or combines—that will come later. For now, we're just looking at scattering seeds. It's not a super refined process, according to this parable. Grab a handful of seeds and throw them around.

That's the easy part, as we will see.

What happened next is a little more complicated and yet is essential for understanding growth. As the sower threw the seeds all about, logically they landed in a diversity of places in which the condition of the soil varied greatly. This may not sound very profound, but I believe it is the crux of the matter. The diversity of the types of soil produced in turn a diversity of outcomes. The seeds were scattered and landed on very different places. And that actually matters most of all.

This feature of the story challenges a fundamental problem with the way we tend to think about *the way people think*. Our default thought process is that everyone processes information and truth in the same ways we do. Now I know that when I say this, each of us thinks we already fully know such a thing. But the truth remains that we live our lives with a subconscious, unspoken assumption that everyone around us is seeing the world—and truth—through the same lenses as our own.

The proof is found in the way we are instinctively offended by others when they differ from us. For example, when someone sitting in a restaurant booth next to you speaks to their server in a harsh and entitled tone, we tend to think, *What is wrong with that jerk?* We hardly ever think to ourselves, *I wonder if the way I've been addressing my server is wrong; maybe that stranger over there knows the right way and I should start screaming because my onion rings are cold.* Instinctively, you believe both you and your seemingly rude neighbor are looking at the situation with your respective servers in exactly the same light and with the same set of culturally accepted values, so you have the right to be offended by the fact that they are breaking the "rules" you assume you both adhere to.

The parable of the sower may seem simple, but it teaches us one of the most hidden-in-plain-sight truths of the world, of the kingdom, and of growth: the "soil" of every person's heart is not the same. All people may be created equal, but all people do not approach the world equally the same. Everyone has a different background and backstory—a different way of perceiving the world. Not all of our lenses are the same, so it makes sense that we don't see the world the same way.

We may know this from a cognitive perspective, but Jesus knows we tend to live our lives offended at those whose "soil" is different from our own. And from a church perspective, we tend to act as if there is a single method for helping to produce growth in a diversity of people. It is a haughty viewpoint that we don't even realize we have. Jesus' story is meant to help us see that all soils—that is, the hearts of people—are not in the same state of being. If we don't understand this simple point, we will have both unrealistic and unmet expectations. Everyone has a different *backstory*—so now *back to the story*.

WHAT THE SEEDS ALWAYS DO

Jesus said that when the sower tossed the seeds, some of them fell on a path. For all intents and purposes, it was a sidewalk. It was basically unturned, unsowable, worn, hard ground. The seeds lay there for a few minutes until the birds of the air came and snatched them away.

The second scattering of seeds fell on ground riddled with stones. Since they made their way into the soil, plants sprung up quickly—a hopeful beginning. But because of all the rocks, the roots ran out of room and the plants became scorched in the hot sun, withering and dying.

The third batch of seeds also fell on dirt, but they were like parts of my backyard—seeds among the thorns. In this case, the seeds took root and grew to a mature size. After all, the soil was good enough ground for the thorns, so it was good enough for something to grow. More on that soon.

Finally, the fourth scattering of the seeds fell on good soil. They grew—a lot. They produced a lot of fruit. They worked as intended. In fact, they worked just like seeds are designed to work *if* they find the right kind of soil. And within that huge "if" is where I believe the majority of our work resides.

The sower stays the same, and the seeds are presumably the same seeds. The *different types of soil* are the real focus of the parable. I think this realization is most easily seen in the third scattering—in the seeds among thorns. We will cover this particular scenario in depth in chapter 7, but I want to reference this one in particular here for the purpose of pointing out some of the notions we may have regarding the process of sowing and the roles of everyone and everything involved. You see, there is an assumption that every seed in the story dies except for that which fell on the good ground, but this isn't at all what Jesus said. It is much more complex than just one set of people being "all bad" and another set of people being "all good."

We often want to view the world through black-and-white lenses. But as Jesus points out, people have a lot more complexity to their lives than we like to admit, as any of us who have children know. My daughters don't grow into maturity in all areas at once. They grow in stages, and often they grow differently and at different rates than their sibling counterparts. One may struggle emotionally in an area that another seems to master easily. To that end, the worst thing you can do is place one-size-fits-all expectations on people whose emotions, dispositions, struggles, and strengths have so many vast differences. The same is true with the way seeds grow differently in different types of soil.

I wonder if a lot of churches have grown a "seeds among thorns" culture. As I've worked with many churches to help revamp their culture, I always ask them about the growth happening in a culture of choke. You see it in the culture of the insider—that is, in a language and general attitude predominantly skewed to those who are already there, to the detriment of those who are not. This kind of church can grow rapidly on its own without proper tending, kingdom purpose, or biblical vision. Too many churches have experienced this kind of growth, cultivating their own unique cultural DNA that is mostly only accessible from the inside and not the outside.

Much like the weeds in my yard, when I merely trim off the top of whatever is already growing, regardless of its substance, things can actually look pretty good from a distance. Properly presented, seedlings and thorns can appear to be green and lush. In our personal lives, we may be doing okay at our job, holding it together in our marriage, or maybe even going to church almost every week. As churches, we may able to pay our monthly bills and staff salaries, own a debt-free facility, and pull off a pretty good list of surprisingly good programs every week. The yard is green and growing.

There is nothing necessarily wrong with any of these in isolation, but they shouldn't be occurring in isolation because we should never be in isolation—the good seed of the gospel says so. Our lives and our churches are meant for so much more, and the right kind of seed is the key. All of these "green" things together can paint the picture from a distance of something that appears to be alive and vibrant. But we must honestly ask ourselves, "Are we really growing in healthy ways?"

As we explore what real life is supposed to look like from the perspective of the One who designed us for it, we are invited to lean into stories like these so we can honestly evaluate what's really there. Regardless of the size of our congregations, do they contain fully devoted disciples who are experiencing nothing less than real, actual, crazy transformation in honest, authentic community each and every day of the week, not just on Sundays?

Or are we experiencing static existence, routine religion, and a faith that is wrecking no one in truly supernatural ways?

Remember that the crazy thing about the seeds among thorns is that the seeds actually grew. They produced *foliage* but lacked *fruitfulness*. When there's not a lot of fruit to speak of, we tend to speak instead about the appearance of this foliage. We redirect to the growth we do have. We mow it evenly and declare, "See, this looks just as good as our neighbor's yard!"

For some, ministry has become more about winning the prize for the greenest lawn in town rather than the healthiest lawn. It can easily be more about seeing the numbers increase than seeing lives transformed by the change that only God can make happen. We love to promote the way our church functions versus the way other churches function. We have *this* speaker. *This* worship team. *This* program. *This* building. Soon enough, our mindset quickly becomes very introverted, with a lot of navel-gazing taking place.[4]

But if only we could be honest enough to pull out the thorns and weeds of whatever amount of fruitless activities we're focusing on in the name of "church life," we would see that all that may remain is some patchy dirt with very little real grass growing—and not a lot of actual life, at least as it's defined biblically. The seeds were scattered here, but the choke of thorns has left us barren of any real fruitfulness.

I'm not trying to be overly critical here, nor do I want to castigate other preachers or Jesus' bride. I only hope to offer honest reflection. The truth is each of our yards will grow thorns and weeds if left to their own devices. My yard—my life and my church—doesn't have some different, more superior soil. We are not gurus; we are broken, just like the people we are working to make room for. We all have dirt that needs to be turned over, cultivated, and purified. We all have thorns. But the good news—and consequently, *the* Good News—is that we all have the same God-created potential for the same God-initiated transformation to occur. Jesus wants to wreck your life and church, just as much as he wants to wreck mine.

In the next chapter, we'll look at the various kinds of soil Jesus refers to in this parable; but for now, it suffices to say that the soil always matters—and that the seeds always work. They grew in every type of soil except the hardened soil, but they weren't allowed to stay and sink into that dirt because the birds came and stole them away. If they could have gotten through the hardness, they would have grown.

It's great news to know that everything Jesus sows into the hearts of people always has the potential to work. These days, we are almost afraid just to share the gospel with our churches—or perhaps even say the word *gospel* in the first place. It begins to sound antiquated to us, but this story reminds us of the central truth of life and growth: it all begins with the message of hope found in Jesus Christ. The gospel is not just a Romans Road map to salvation or an EvangeCube. The gospel is "living and active, sharper than any two-edged sword, piercing to the division of soul and of spirit, of joints and of marrow, and discerning the thoughts and intentions of the heart."[5] It is also "the power of God for salvation to everyone who believes, to the Jew first and also to the Greek."[6]

Let this sink into your own soil for a minute. Besides the gospel of Jesus Christ himself, nothing else in all of Scripture is called the "power of God" to save all people.[7] I'm not talking about *just* the details of the virgin birth, the crucifixion, and the resurrection. When I talk about the gospel, I'm referring to the Spirit-inspired understanding of the way the very incarnated love of God became human and lived among us, defeated what has always defeated us, and paid the price we could never afford.

This is not your average bumper sticker slogan or church marquee gospel. I'm talking about the good news of the risen Christ, which is "foolishness to those who are perishing, but to us who are being saved it is the power of God."[8]

I encourage you, regardless of your church's size, demographics, tradition, or context, to empty your life, ministry, and church of any and all confidence in anything other than the gospel—the Word of God expressed in the Son of God and revealed to hearts through the Spirit of God. This is a cultural action, not a practical one. It is a matter of ethos reflective of a true belief that Christ does the work that matters in the hearts of people and in building his church.

I love pastors, and I learn from them every day. I know no pastors or Christians in this world who would disagree that Jesus is the one who changes lives and builds the church. Most of us think we believe this, but I'm not sure we really do. I have to fight this struggle in my own psyche at times. If I'm not careful, the pursuits, energies, and security (or lack thereof) of my daily life and our church's culture can demonstrate otherwise. We may *think we believe* that God brings the growth, but we can fall into the trap of *actually believing* it is mostly up to us. It can happen so fast and can cause us to keep the focus on our gifts, talents, expressions, structure, facilities, and the like—on those things that make us unique and different from other churches and thus make us the center of the whole process.

A gospel-centered perspective and culture choose not to emphasize what makes us different from all other churches, but rather what is supposed to make us the same: the work of Jesus to continually transform our lives and this world. I love you enough to ask you the honest question: Is this message of the gospel the primary emphasis of the church context in which you lead or are a member? Or is it about how much better your preacher can preach, your singers can sing, your children's ministry can produce events, or a hundred other "distinctives" by which most churches identify themselves and seek to attract new people? If we grow by anything other than the real gospel at work in real people's hearts—which means we must first focus on believing and revealing our own brokenness that proves we are also real people—then, as we will see in the next chapter, our growth will either be unsustainable or will include a lot of other things with it that choke out its effectiveness, its fruitfulness.

Before we understand anything else about growth, we must put our full confidence in the gospel. We must return to this place every day as individuals and leaders and remind our churches of the only One who does the transforming in others, and that we are the ones who constantly receive the transformation. Regardless of how hard we work at a thousand different endeavors related to Jesus and his church, the truth that actually changes lives is that the seeds of the gospel are what always work.

I encourage you to push yourself past the familiar Christian language of these statements and ask yourself these questions: As I make an honest evaluation of my own attitude, efforts, and the general culture of my church, are we really living as if the "seeds" of Christ and his gospel are the only possible means of real transformation in people's lives, from the lead pastor to the newest guest in the parking lot? If we asked a stranger to visit our website, drive onto our properties, sit in our services, and audit our leadership meetings, would they conclude, without any extra coaching or leading language from us, that surely Christ and his message are the keys to changed lives? Would that seed be so noticeable, or would they marvel at our systems, our talents, our facilities, and our resources—testaments to what can happen when good leaders get together in high-potential and high-capacity communities?

These are hard but necessary questions to ask. They lead us to understand our central role in the process, which, as I said in the opening line of this chapter, is *not* to change lives. We could never do so, no matter how hard we worked, so it's important to figure out what kind of work is actually ours to do as his church.

CHAPTER 6

TURNING OVER THE SOIL

We Don't Turn Hearts;
We Do Turn Over Heart Soil

H ave you ever sat down for a heart-to-heart conversation with someone, only to realize that while they are shaking their heads up and down, they have no clue what you're really trying to say? This was an experience Jesus appeared to have almost every day with people all around him. Again, this is one of the reasons he predominantly used parables—stories and allegories—to communicate what was essentially a foreign culture to them. They were hearing the words coming out of his mouth but were usually completely incapable of comprehending the bigger picture he was painting for them.

It's important for us to understand that we live with a cultural context defined by our time in history, the places we are from and in which we currently live, and a host of other factors. For Jesus' disciples and for us, comprehending the culture of the kingdom of God is akin to trying to discern the meaning of a foreign language and then learning to speak it. Like visiting a foreign country and trying to order food off a menu at a local café, the barriers of language and culture can be frustrating and overwhelming. They are foreign.

Such is the culture of God's kingdom, but it's not really the language that is foreign; it's the ethic. The way God sees the world is generally inverted from the way we see it. Obviously, we are the ones who are upside down, not him. We can even speak the language from the menu, using religious-sounding, theological terms to try to project some level of fluency in God's ways. But just like someone who makes up sounds to fake his or her way through foreign language, such actions just make us seem less authentic, not more.

As disciples, the real culture of Christ's kingdom is something we must know is foreign to us so we will continually approach God's ways with humility, never assuming we are heavenly fluent while we live on earth. In other words, we have to remember we are growing in his ethic and never arrive to it fully in this life. Oddly enough, this humility is a part of the kingdom ethic—it speaks volumes to our hearts, as well as to the culture around us.

Such a posture refuses to sum up Jesus' ways with cutesy aphorisms and acrostics for the purpose of calling the whole matter closed. We remain open to the gospel because we know that it remains infinitely higher than us, perpetually calling us to daily transformation. We never arrive, so we can joyfully expect to spend all of our lives learning the language of the kingdom of heaven—that is, the one much higher than mere words. But if you're not fluent quite yet, you're in good company. Jesus' own disciples weren't speaking it fluently either.

It's easy to be pretty hard on Jesus' disciples, what with all of them arguing over which of them will be the greatest in Jesus' kingdom[1] and then trying to rain down fire out of heaven on a village that rejected them,[2] and one of Jesus' best friends disowning him three times[3] in a profanity-laden rant right after slicing off a dude's ear.[4] Don't forget the one who absolutely refused to believe in the resurrection of Jesus until he could literally put his hand inside Jesus' gaping wound.[5] Of course, the coup de grâce was Judas siphoning a little off the top from the treasury and ultimately selling out Jesus for thirty pieces of silver.[6] These guys had some serious issues.

But the biblical record of Jesus' telling of the parable of the sower reveals that the disciples had gotten something right. They knew enough to know they weren't understanding what Jesus was saying. So they had the wherewithal to simply keep coming to him and asking for deeper explanations. Again, this is the posture of a disciple—to keep reminding oneself that Jesus' ways are infinitely higher than our own, so we must keep asking him to reveal deeper heights to our lowly state of understanding.

Being either ridiculously confused by his profound story or being very moved by it, the disciples came to him and asked for more. This is what we must do as well. Just as he did for them, he will always respond to us with a yes. This is the process of learning word by word, ethic by ethic, sentiment by sentiment what the kingdom of our sovereign God is truly like. And with every transformative experience, we gain a little more fluency.

THE DEAL WITH SOWERS

"Hear then the parable of the sower: When anyone hears the word of the kingdom and does not understand it, the evil one comes and snatches away what has been sown in his heart. This is what was sown along the path. As for what was sown on rocky ground, this is the one who hears the word and immediately receives it with joy, yet he has no root in himself, but endures for a while, and when tribulation or persecution arises on account

of the word, immediately he falls away. As for what was sown among thorns, this is the one who hears the word, but the cares of the world and the deceitfulness of riches choke the word, and it proves unfruitful. As for what was sown on good soil, this is the one who hears the word and understands it. He indeed bears fruit and yields, in one case a hundredfold, in another sixty, and in another thirty."

Matthew 13:18–23

Jesus perfectly explained the story he had just told them, but just as is true with all of God's Word, this explanation itself will keep us busy constantly realigning ourselves with his kingdom for the rest of our lives. In fact, I believe that embedded in his explanation are many of the deepest secrets of the work of the church—of course, it's not supposed to be a secret since it is written right here in red letter. Again, the "growth secrets" we really want are about how to *fill the seats with people*, but the growth secrets Jesus offers us are about our role in the process by which he *fills people's hearts with eternal life*.

The parable of the sower is a radical departure from anything people had ever heard about the way God works in the hearts of people. So much so that even though the disciples were probably amening him publicly, they were still completely confused. Again, we may know this story well, but I wonder how many of us struggle, thinking we're doing good soil work. After all, when it comes to church metrics, we are covered in terms of "butts and budgets," that is, solid attendance and adequate financial resources.

In private, Jesus offers a more in-depth description for those willing to ask—hopefully that includes you and me. Jesus begins his deeper explanation by defining the seeds, the identities and roles of all the characters, and the nature of the soil. Remember what we acknowledged earlier: the sower is the preacher; the seeds are the word of the kingdom, and the soil is the heart of people. I find it fascinating that in this story, two things never changed—the sower and the seeds. We've already talked about why the seeds of the gospel are not changing, but the sower seems to be a different matter in our modern context.

In most of our contexts, we would immediately identify the sower as the pastor, the Bible teacher, or the preacher. The leader, the pastor who shares God's message both with church folks and with those outside the church walls—they are the sower of the seeds of the word of God's kingdom. In the parable, along with the seeds that never change, the sower is the steady figure. They are faithful in their sowing; they don't change. In the farming industry, the seeds are cheap and the sower works for free, especially if you own the farm. Plus, the job is simple—scatter the seeds.

In most of our churches, this is not the case—the sower is one of the most complicated and expensive parts of the process. There is a general expectation that if we can just get that preacher to do right; preach better; become more attractive with his work ethic, balance of ministry and family, humor, intellectual prowess, and social engagement online; and be seen at all the coffee shops, ball fields, and hospitals in town, then the church will grow and be successful. And if he or she can't or won't do this, we're going to trade them in for a better sower. This is why the profession of vocational ministry is one of the most unstable in our culture, with people changing jobs and moving to another church in another town as regularly as one changes the water filter in a refrigerator.

We put so much energy into the role of the sower, but it is significant to note that in this parable, Jesus did not. The sower was simply the distributor of the seeds we know are essential to transformation. Let me be clear—it is absolutely necessary that the seeds be scattered.

Pastors, I want to say something specifically to you for a moment. Everyone else, please listen in because you should know this too. Pastor, let me encourage you by insulting you a bit—and if you will endure it, you will surely be encouraged. I promise. I know that your name is on the church marquee; your photo is on your church's website; and your ministry friends refer to the church where you pastor as "your church." But in terms of the process of real transformation in the hearts of people, you are merely and primarily and simply and significantly . . . a seed thrower. That's it. And *that's it*! That's what you get to do! You may think that as a speaker, motivator, or leader, you throw the seeds much better than other sowers, but in the culture of Christ's kingdom, this is a ridiculous and worthless comparison. Take the seeds and get them out as far and wide as you can throw them.

Can you imagine the lightness—the freedom—you would feel if you refused to play the imaginary part everyone in your church and town keeps insisting you take on? I understand that some of us feel we have no choice. Elder boards, committees, and members demand certain things of us—and some of us don't have other staff members to share the load. However, even these pressures reveal that the people in our churches don't necessarily understand the elements of the seeds and the role of the sower as Jesus described them. You may have to be busy and even face numerous stressors, but unbiblical (or at least extrabiblical) expectations that crush the leader's soul shouldn't be one of them.

What if you didn't wake up tomorrow morning with the weight of the whole church and others' expectations on you, truly feeling that if you don't please, educate, entertain, or appease the people with your best efforts, they will transfer to the church across town—or worse, they will not make it to heaven? I think that sowers often get themselves confused with the seeds, which is a tragic trade no one can sustain or endure. As church attenders, we sometimes confuse our pastors with the seeds as well.

We have much more ground to cover here about the pastor's role and also the true nature of kingdom stewardship, but it all begins with understanding the role God intends for the pastor in terms of preaching—to rightly distribute the truth of Christ's gospel. Enjoy this assignment. It is sacred. It is important. It is prophetic. It is laborious. It is simply profound. Listen, if you think I'm downplaying your role or if this offends your sense of self-importance and pride, I say let it be slain—it's killing you anyway, whether you realize it or not.

It's also beneficial to momentarily expand your viewpoint of the one who sows seeds because, biblically, this is God's assignment for everyone who belongs to this kingdom, not just the preacher, or more specifically the pastor/teacher. Each of us is called to be prophetic, and I don't mean this in the sense that many people interpret the term, which focuses on the use and application of a charismatic spiritual gift or manifestation.

First Corinthians 14:24–25 encourages all of us to live in the prophetic, specifically through the communication of the message of Christ and his rescue mission for all people. This is about our willingness to always be scattering the seeds—the word of the kingdom—as we walk through life. This is not about a witnessing program or a series of conversations with strangers that we train people to have, though these types of things can be helpful in certain contexts. I'm talking about a different kind of prophetic, Christ-centered living, where the expression of the hope of the message of Christ is naturally being both lived and shared as a way of life—in a way that it is compelling and attractive to those who hear rather than forced and awkward, as it so often is.

One of my favorite modern examples of this is Pastor Chris Hodges. His life, his message, his writings, his habits, and his actions are consistently expressive of the Christ-centered confession he has. He lives to make Jesus known and to help people grow closer to him. One of the signs that a person is living prophetically is they compel you to draw closer to Jesus—to be a stronger Christian. Every time I read his books, hear him preach, or sit in a room with him, I'm inspired to go all in with Jesus. He's not the only one I could name here, but he's been such a gift to my life. Thankfully the body of Christ has many people to grow under and learn from.

Prophetic, seed-scattering living is what the apostle Paul aspired to when he said in Acts 20:24 that the only thing that mattered to him was to tell everyone he met about the extravagant generosity of God in Christ. Some people think of sharing the gospel as standing on the curb with a megaphone yelling at those who pass by—which is a method Jesus never used. People were attracted to him—and they came to him in droves.

I know what you're thinking. Jesus had miracles in his pocket, so no wonder he could draw a crowd (though obviously sharing the gospel isn't necessarily about drawing a crowd). There is some validity to this, but we act as if Jesus doesn't have the ability to continue to do incredible things that will draw people today—and I don't just mean what we generally consider to be miraculous, things like healing, exorcisms, and the like. He still does these things, but even these things didn't keep the crowds—at one point, they all abandoned him, even though they knew he could perform miracles.[7] Miracles weren't Jesus' missional focal point because he knew they weren't enough to transform hearts, which is why he almost always commanded those who had just experienced miracles to seek deeper things of the kingdom (go and sin no more; go present yourself before the priest; go back to the town and tell everyone what God has done for you; and so forth).

It was Jesus' daily life spent with the disciples that transformed their hearts, preparing them for the work of the Holy Spirit and the subsequent mission of carrying this gospel to all the world, as well as the suffering they would endure at every turn. His collective, conversational interaction and relationship with them comprised the seeds that produced supernatural fruit in them. In fact, he explicitly told them it would be his words and kingdom ways shaping their ongoing relationships within a grace-first community that would prove to the world they were his disciples[8]—and just as importantly, that being a disciple is the life anyone in this world should desire.

The proof would not be in how well they could preach. Paul was a great preacher but awfully long-winded! He once preached so long that a dude fell asleep and fell out of a window to his death.[9] I'm guessing his sermon lacked a few funny stories, alliteration, and a catchy logo. Again, the proof was not found in the quality of their sermon delivery.

It was also not found in how many people would attend their churches, how many books they would write, or even how kind they would be to strangers. In fact, it would not be the way *they treated the world* that would create the transformation of the world; rather, it would be *the world watching the way they treated one another* that would be the irresistible evidence everyone still clamors for today. In other words, real disciples living real life together are sowers of something more powerful than themselves, living authentically in love for one another regardless of who is watching—and consequently, Christ promises to make sure that the world will be watching, which often backfires on us instead of being the thing we should most expect and desire.

Are you beginning to see how the principle of being sowers

works? Our words, relationships, and attitudes are already sowing something into others, with or without our intentionality or consent. You are already a sower, scattering what matters the most in your life. The life of a true, honest, confessional, authentic community of believers (by the way, this should be a standard definition of every single church) is the living reflection of the gospel that we're supposed to be scattering all the time, not just when we stop to witness or preach. As Paul wrote, "To live is Christ."[10]

A witness is merely someone who can accurately describe someone or something they have actually seen and experienced. The best witnesses don't need to be articulate, dazzling the courtroom with spectacular descriptions that bring everyone to laughter or tears. Such theatrics are immaterial to the accuracy of the testimony and can even distract from the truth. The best witness is the one who experienced something and can talk about it with clarity and accuracy.

Such are the sowers we should all be—people who are experiencing something. This rings just as true for pastors and preachers as it does for every Christian, if not more so. We've overcomplicated the sowing process, elevating the sower above the seeds and then skipping the real, hard, fulfilling work of the kingdom we should be doing as his church—preparing the soil of the hearts of the hearers. Now comes my favorite reality of this parable and the best church growth strategy I can offer.

INVESTING IN THE DIRT

We know we are to be scattering seeds, and when we scatter the right seeds, they work every time, because the work of sowing is God's work, not our own. We know it really doesn't matter who does the scattering, so we shouldn't elevate the preacher to an unhealthy degree—yes, human leadership matters, but it is not what transforms a life or produces the right kind of growth among people. I'm not disregarding pastors and ministry leaders, but just reminding us that we have a role to scatter and to steward what has been given to us.

So where does this leave us? We are on the cusp of the real fruitful work of the church that leads to the right kind of growth. We plant and we water, but God brings the growth. But if we dig down in that sequence and connect it to the parable of the sower, we find a process before the planting and the watering that many of us as leaders and members either downplay or ignore altogether—and doing so actually keeps us from experiencing the right kind of growth. I believe this is the key to healthy growth in your church. It's not a formula; it's a process. It's not a program; it's an ever-present culture. It's not a curriculum; it's an ethic.

I'm talking about the process of preparing the soil. Don't miss this part.

As in my yard, a certain procedure is required before the seeds can take root, no matter how high quality the seeds are and how skilled the sower is. In fact, this is where most of the hard work on our part really happens—preparing and turning over the soil and making room for the seeds to take root in fertile, arable ground.

Every farmer—and every weekend yard warrior—knows that the most expensive part of getting a field or a flowerbed to produce the right kind of plants is the work that must be done *to* the dirt. Seeds are literally *dirt* cheap. You can sow an acre of corn for less than thirty dollars' worth of seeds—you will be hard-pressed to find any other profession where the investment portion of the equation is quite so proportionately low. And if we stick with the current metaphor of this parable, the odds are that the laborers were family members working on land owned by the family's father, which meant they were working the land for free. So the seeds are cheap and the sowers aren't expensive—they should freely want to expend energy on sowing to the right soil.

If you've ever worked on your own landscaping, you know what requires the most money, effort, energy. You can spend twenty dollars on plants at Lowe's for your little backyard project. Easy, right? Wrong—because it then takes twelve hours of back-breaking labor to till the ground, construct the frames for your raised beds, plant the seeds, add topsoil, add organic compost, perhaps add a top layer of mulch, add plenty of fertilizer and water, and then put up fencing to keep out the critters. And after the initial labor is done, you won't have much time to rest. It will take hours upon hours of continual watering, watching, weeding, adding Miracle-Gro, and a host of other energy expenditures to keep the soil sustained in a condition where the seeds can do their work.

Most of the time and money are *in the dirt, not the seeds and not the sower.* Catch this: the primary energy of a healthy and kingdom-growing church is spent on cultivating, turning, rehabbing, preparing, and keeping the soil of the hearts of people sustained. So at LifePoint Church, we've decided to invest a lot in the dirt.

From a commercial farming perspective, farmers and companies spend millions upon millions of dollars on massive machines to work the dirt—that is, to turn it over, remove rocks, remove weeds, aerate, fertilize, treat for pests, irrigate, and so forth. Every effective, professional farmer understands how to get the ground ready, how to rest a field, how to rotate crops based on the nutrient composition of the dirt, and when to start the process of prepping the ground in order to sow the plants with enough time to yield the greatest harvest. He or she also understands that the best seeds and the most expert staff still cannot force the seeds to produce any better than God's timing and God's providence. The best seeds don't change the amount of rain and sunshine that will come—God does that. The greatest sower and laborers cannot guarantee that a crop will yield enough to produce good margins—God does that.

But what they can do is get the dirt ready and keep the dirt healthy. This is why we serve people, open doors (both literally and figuratively), rock their babies, smile a lot, practice extreme generosity, and preach in a way that is life-giving and challenging. All of the activities of our church are motivated by preparing the ground, turning the dirt, removing the rocks, and pushing back the weeds that choke out life. Everything we do is motivated by this parable, and we spend a considerable amount of resources and energy to get the soil of every person ready to receive the seeds of God's word.

I think of Margie, affectionately known as our "cookie lady." She is probably one of the most servant-hearted people I've ever met. I won't share her age, but know she is a "seasoned saint." And in her first year at LifePoint, she quickly took over the entire process of providing fresh-baked chocolate chip cookies for our first-time guests. Every weekend, she spends hours preparing, baking, sorting, bagging, and praying over the small baggies that each contain four delicious cookies.

It's a tedious, time-consuming novelty that has become a cultural fit for our church and is even anticipated by many first-time guests who heard about it before their visit. In fact, countless people have come to our church to visit because they heard about the kids ministry, the preaching, the friendly people, and also the rumor that you get homemade cookies on your first visit! Margie knows that the purpose of the cookies is simple: they soften hardened hearts, help lift the rocks from the stony ground of the hearts of the undiscipled, show hope and joy to the stressed-out person living with a heart of thorns, and become a welcome treat to enjoy while the sower stands on the platform scattering seeds. (Yes, we encourage guests to eat their cookies during the service.)

So then, when it comes to growth in an individual or in a church, our main role is to create the spaces and the environments through the establishment of the right culture and the right systems or processes that reflect the heart of the Father revealed in the gospel. Such work can help foster room within someone for the right things to grow—and the wrong things to die away or, more accurately, be cut away. The seeds work every time. The sower should be ready to do his or her work in the process. The real work of the church is in the dirt, helping to prepare the hearts of people for the transformative life only the seeds can produce in them.

Coming full circle to a concept I introduced earlier, from this perspective we can and should stop assuming that everyone who encounters the church either out in the community or in their workplace or chooses to come to a service when the church gathers on Sundays is ready to process the seeds of the gospel in the same way as everyone else. They are not, so we must do the work of dealing with their hearts from a place of sensitivity, empathy, and intentionality as we abandon a one-size-fits-all approach to the way we *do church*. On the contrary, *being the church* means being purposeful about placing value in the process of dealing with people's hearts, being aware because of the explicit truth found in parables such as these that the condition of various hearts is a matter of vast diversity.

Some viewpoints within Christianity lead us to believe that good soil is the only soil that matters because it is the only one that survived and produced fruit in the story. In other words, we should only focus on those whose hearts are perfectly ready for the gospel. I think this is a dangerous perspective that is contrary to the heart of the Father—the heart that never stopped sowing seeds of hope for a wayward, hard-hearted kid lost in a foreign land. Good soil is worked soil. If it isn't worked and cleared out and prepared, it develops weeds, rocks, or pathways. Good soil is only one of the four types mentioned to be fruitful. But with the right work and investment, any of the soil types can become good ground!

Devoted Christians should acknowledge that *each type of soil has value.* In fact, this is where I believe the main work of the church is revealed, a work that so many within her circles seem confused and misguided about. But if we can grasp this truth regarding the soil, we can get to work with the right attitude toward a godly aim. The bottom line is that it just takes more work to get hard, rocky, and thorny soil to become good soil— and that's the good work the church should be doing. It's why we do everything we can to be a church where anyone is welcome— because we are pleading with God to have the opportunity to deal with some hard hearts, some stony hearts, some hearts that are choked by the thorns of life.

In fact, this parable suggests that all "soil types" deserve to have the seeds scattered on them. That means all hearts need the gospel. While it's easier to see a harvest in good soil, that's only one-fourth of the soil types. This means that 75 percent of the people who come into the church we serve who hear the gospel scattered by their local sower will need an army of people who are willing to do whatever it takes to turn some dirt, pull some weeds, and remove some rocks in order to see these seeds become fruitful in their hearts.

As I write these words, I'm looking out over downtown Nashville. Pavement abounds in this concrete jungle, but the truth is, I could get a garden to grow where the sidewalk just below now resides. Is it possible? Sure it is—it will just take a lot of work. I'd have to spend thousands of dollars to break up and remove the asphalt, dig out the gravel and garbage in the dirt below, add topsoil, and then do a dozen more things to get that once hard surface turned into the kind of soil that will produce plants that will produce fruit. Sure, from a practical standpoint, I would rather find some good ground somewhere and plant there. I just mean to say that all soil can be turned over and prepared into the kind of soil that can sustain good growth.

All four soil types in this story matter—we just have to do different work for each one. It is a different process to move rocks than it is to cut away thorns. Thorns require gloves and some sort of sharp blade or cutters, while rocks require gloves and some sort of shovel or hoe. Some thorns may require a whole different set of skills, such as knowing how to treat the plant with chemicals, while chemicals are worthless in the process of removing rocks.

But even when it comes to removing rocks, not all jobs are created equal. If you want to remove a few stones from your garden, that's one thing; but if you want to remove a giant pile of riprap from your ditch, you need bigger equipment and a pickup truck—and maybe a back brace.

Most of us can see all four types of soil in our own group of family and friends. We all know someone who is hard-hearted to the gospel, simply opposed to anything church related. Any conversation you have with them leads not just to disinterest but to active disagreement. Wounds there are deep, so the seeds never even penetrate the top layer. There is a lot of work to do here.

From a church perspective, hard-hearted people are obviously the least likely to come to a church service. Even so, we must always make room for them, just in case. We must focus on a kind of culture that will help soften hard hearts, where we are open to difficult topics of faith, discussing them from the stage, in classes, and in small groups. This means not acting as if everyone out there completely agrees with our perspective. It means we acknowledge that everyone who disagrees with us is not completely worthless or devoid of understanding, and that we should even make room for those who disagree to be free to express their disagreements so we can attempt to understand what's going on in their own particular heart soil.

When they do show up in our church, I still scatter seeds. I'm not going to stop scattering seeds because their hearts are hardened. I'm just going to love them and try to soften—or perhaps even break through—the ground of their hearts. As a church, we will build an entire system and recruit as many volunteers as possible to greet them, welcome them, love on them, serve them, bless their kids, be generous toward them, seat them, lead them, and do whatever we can to work that pavement out of their hearts. This must not be done in a manipulative manner or we will only make hard hearts into granite hearts. Rather, this means we approach people from the Father's heart perspective, engaging in relationships wherein they are valued, whether they ever agree with us or not. This is a hard place to be, but it is the way of the Father and the way he uses us to soften the soil.

Let me remind you that LifePoint Church may be growing larger, but we struggle mightily in these areas, just like anyone who wants to please God with the way they live as his church. I had a pastor compliment "my" church, talking about how awesome we are. I appreciated it, but I let him know in no uncertain terms that this is not "my" church and that we are so very broken, seeking wholeness day by day. We get it wrong sometimes—and sometimes the hard-hearted walk away from us without having become any softer.

We can't control all the outcomes, but we can control our

culture. We can't control the sun or the rain, but we can get inside a tractor and work the dirt. We refuse to stop living as if God has placed a premium on the heart of every person in our city—and even if they can't stand us, we try to keep our processes focused on softening their hearts through kindness, empathy, and the act of listening. Our church contains individuals, couples, and families who say they have felt unwelcome for every reason under the religious sun, so if you've ever heard that complaint in your church, you are not alone. We just keep trying. We don't avoid them, even though they have said hurtful things about us and questioned our methods and our very motives—after all, they say, no megachurch can really be relational or effective since all we care about is shallow growth and money.

We just keep hugging them. We keep engaging them. Yes, we will love them well enough to communicate truth as we do it, but we expect that hearts come in all conditions and that it's God's job to truly transform a life. Young, old, religious, atheist, straight, gay, rich, poor—you name it, each person's soil has a story of how it got the way it is. I think of one young man in our church who is super angry on social media. He's been bullied, so he has put up a pretty big wall toward church. I've never had a breakthrough with him, but I keep showing up in the relationship every time he has the courage to show up in my church. Kind words. Engagement. Follow-up. Expressions of truth and unconditional love, because, after all, truth and love shouldn't be mutually exclusive.

Right now, I'm throwing seeds on a hard sidewalk. This kid's hurt. He's wounded. He's in sin. And he knows it. What now? He still matters to the Father, that's what. And this means he should still matter to us. Is turning over the soil of someone's hard heart the kind of work most churches celebrate? Unfortunately, it's not.

But it can be.

CHAPTER 7

SEEDS AMONG STONES AND THORNS

*The Culture of the Kingdom Prepares
the Soil; Anything Else Spoils It*

As we have learned, there is nothing faulty about the seeds, the sower, or even the process of sowing. What really matters most in terms of our effectiveness is the type of soil—the *condition of the heart of the hearer*. When a person's heart is completely hardened, unturned, and unprepared for any amount or any types of seeds, we must remain prayerfully vigilant in showing the love and truth of Christ with them in wisdom, no matter the outcome. But we see other kinds of soil in the story, which is why we shouldn't approach every soil the same. In the case of the stony ground, the seeds took root and grew quickly. I want to speak to the broader audience of Christians for a moment, not just pastors and leaders.

Seeds among stones. There is a lot of this kind of soil happening in today's church because we are so conversion-driven. We see a lot of fast converts. We want people to get converted and baptized as quickly as possible, but we often fail to be diligent to *keep working* in the soil of their hearts by discipling them into the kind of community that continues to actively turn over the soil in our hearts. In the case of the seeds among the stones, the soil needed to be tended to quickly and consistently, not just one time.

We tend to think that once people have made a profession of faith, are serving on Sundays, and attend a small group meeting at least twice a month that the mission has been accomplished. While these are worthwhile and extremely helpful goals, we must remember that hearts continue to face issues and even change after they have accepted the seeds of the gospel. The battle is not over, which is why a "raise your hand and join a church" mentality of conversion can be an incomplete way to approach the growth of people's souls, much less a church.

When we toss people into the lush, green weeds of a church experience without continually tending to the condition of their hearts, there can be little room for their roots to really take. So many times, their faith withers and dies when the first season of difficulty or real pressure comes, which is exactly what Jesus said would happen: "This is the man who hears the word . . . yet he has no firm root in himself, but is only temporary, and when affliction or persecution arises because of the word, immediately he falls away."[1] There may be room for the seeds to sprout and spring up, but if we don't engage in the process of making room for these roots to deepen, much like a house built on the sand,[2] we may be able to stand for a while, but we cannot withstand the harsh winds of difficulty that blow against us.

I hope this hasn't been the case for you, but we've noticed many stony-hearted stories in our church—again, we're still learning to be wise farmers in a diversity of soil settings. These are often young Christians—in spiritual, not chronological age. They tend to get saved, go through the classes, and then quickly jump on every volunteer team they can find.

Quite often, these are prodigals who come to themselves and

want to get back home to the safety of the Father, but their first inclination (like the younger brother) is to work their way back into his good graces. They show up repentant and ready to work as a servant, but instead of encountering the heart of the Father that ignores their desires to earn, they encounter church leaders who are pretty burned-out themselves and thrilled to have warm bodies coming through the doors who are willing to actually do something at the church.

As leaders, we must elevate the divine call to tend to the soil of people's hearts above our own desires to stuff the volunteer stat sheets or alleviate our own overcrowded workload. Over the past ten years, after seeing young believers spring up quickly but then fade away just as fast, we had to learn to adjust on the fly. We began asking ourselves, *How do we love well a young, zealous Christian?* We must pay attention to what's happening in their heart soil, which sometimes leads us to tell them to pump the brakes a bit. We lead them away from the isolating effects of trying to earn a good standing with the Father through hard work and instead compel them to become a part of the authentic community God desires for them, where they are known and know others fully and without shame.

For some, this has meant spending time in community with individuals or couples older and further along in the faith than they are—people who can teach them to pray, to study the Bible, and to remain steady in the faith. Everything is so new and exciting to them, which is something we don't want to squelch or dampen.

Even so, the *brand-new way* of walking still needs *an ancient path* on which to walk. "Thus says the LORD: 'Stand by the roads, and look, and ask for the ancient paths, where the good way is; and walk in it, and find rest for your souls. But they said, "We will not walk in it."'"[3] The New Living Translation says,

"Stop at the crossroads." A new life in Christ is at the epicenter of a crossroads—a choice that leads to many more choices to continue walking in a completely different direction from the one walked before.

The heart of the new believer can often desire the newest, fastest, busiest way. As leaders, we have had to learn to say, "No, you need to slow down and take this ancient path. You need to learn and be trained in community with other believers."

Community is such a buzzword in Christian circles today that I urge you not to skip past what I'm saying because your church already does small groups. After all, being in a community group is not the equivalent of being in community, even though it should be. By definition, community will require being in some sort of group of people, and much of our role as the church should be to help these kinds of groups find one another, be organized, and ultimately pursue discipleship together.

Hear me: community is the biblical context for making disciples, and there is no alternative. Good teaching can't replace it. Miracles can't overshadow it. And an abundance of programs that dazzle the beholder won't reduce its need even one iota. Caring for one another, sharpening one another, admonishing one another, counseling one another, praying for one another, encouraging one another, providing for one another, eating with one another—if you search the "one anothers" of Scripture, you will find that these practices deepen the soil of every believer, helping each of us become fruitful. Notice I didn't mention "exhausting one another." A healthy community life will remove the stones of immaturity and deepen the soil of our spiritual life, helping us avoid works-based theology and isolationist tendencies.

When people have quick responses to faith, religion has often taught them that an "altar" experience will suffice. This is a Charles Finney-esque, revivalist responsiveness that calls people to raise their hands, move down front, and then think that all will be well moving forward.[4] Obviously, there is a moment when we receive the seeds and they find a home in us—and this moment is huge, so I'm not against these kinds of things. I'm only against substituting this for the lifelong process of making disciples—of continuing to tend to the soil, which is the church's main call. We should not make people feel eternally secure while neglecting to help them develop more depth in their discipleship. Such methods are a total mishandling of the people God has brought to our churches.

Emotional responses can be good, but they are also not sustainable. I have a friend whose heart is moved by Easter pageants and missional appeals. He always responds with great gusto, but a few weeks later, he's back to living in a lukewarm state with no real depth. Why? Because he doesn't follow up his momentary step by continuing to walk the ancient path of discipleship, which is the path of grace-first belief leading to real, sustainable, biblical community.

At LifePoint, we endeavor to not just be a church *with* small groups that we call community, but we want to be a church *of* people in real community who choose to intentionally meet in groups. I often tell our church that Sunday may be the *biggest* thing we do, but the *best* thing we do is life in groups. Since our beginning almost a decade ago, we have legitimately reoriented our entire church around the deepening discipleship that can only happen in community, which means everything from our kids and student ministries to our volunteer teams, small groups, and missionary endeavors. We hope that everything we do revolves around Christ-centered community. We believe doing life in community is not just the *best* way to live the Christian life; we believe it's the *only* way to live the Christian life if one wants to bear the fruit Jesus said we should produce.

And like everything that is eternal, this is not an accomplishable mission in terms of being finished one day on this earth, so we are constantly learning, growing, failing, succeeding, and trying again, all within the immeasurable expanses of God's grace.

SEEDS AMONG THORNS (AND WEEDS)

As promised in chapter 5, I'm returning to these particular seeds—the seeds sown among thorns—to point out a few different perspectives regarding their particular placement in the story among the other types of soils and as they more specifically relate to the individuals who come into our churches.

Interestingly enough, another type of seed should be mentioned before we dive into the seeds among thorns again—the seeds among weeds. This comes from the parable directly following the parable of the sower. Jesus talked about another field of good seeds that was vandalized one night by an enemy who sowed weeds among the good seeds. The result was a lot of good growth, but also a lot of weeds. So did the owner of the field rip everything out, including the good seeds? No, he allowed them to grow together, commanding that the good and bad be separated later when the end of the harvest comes.

I mention the seeds among weeds with the seeds among thorns to make the point that both vividly demonstrate there are times when good things grow alongside bad things, sharing the same soil—and in the case of the seeds among thorns, competing for the same nutrient-rich life beneath. Remember that these seeds actually grow; they just don't grow alone. As it is with stony-ground persons, this person experiences a moment of conversion but becomes limited in their fruitfulness and vitality by something else that constantly chokes them out—the cares of this world.

This experience is huge within modern culture, just as it obviously was in Jesus' day. However, I wonder how the disciples would have felt if they could have envisioned wristwatches, iPhones, and coffee makers that brew a cup of energy before you ever wake up because you already know you're going to run out of it.

The cares of this world are the biggest robbers of fruitfulness in our churches today. We are not just surrounded on the outside by these things; we are also filled up on the inside, which explains why we are so overworked, anxiety-prone, and generally unable to cope with the pace and pressures of modern life. Busyness, kids, career—these are just a few of everything this world has to offer but also demands of us. We build churches that are full of programs, systems, and ultimately baggage that just become the new cares of this world—and we call it church programming.

In such a society, church leaders still wonder why people struggle just to *show up*, much less to *grow up*. The weeds and thorns of their own cares, as well as the ones the church sometimes unintentionally adds to them, are literally choking out their fruitfulness. Over time, they become unwitting victims of the *condition of their own hearts*.

But don't get me wrong—the people whose hearts fall into this category (and my bet is that we've all been there at some point in our lives) are not bad, immature, shallow people. They are not monsters; they are trying to be heroes.

I have a friend whose heart is often experiencing seeds among thorns. He is a well-paid professional who works sixty-plus hours a week—a good guy just trying to provide for and bless his family. I know a single mom who works like crazy and makes sure she's at every soccer practice. I have friends who have no choice but to care for their sick, invalid grandparent. And let's not forget the many soldiers who are a part of LifePoint Church who live under incredible pressure with their deployment schedules, often facing death and the carnage of war.

Do you hear what I am saying? These are not bad people who set out to become nominal, fruitless Christians. We can remove that stigma from this story. The real lesson here is simple and applies to all of us equally: the cares of our lives (even the well-intended ones) tend to choke out the ongoing growth the gospel is trying to produce in us.

This story is not referring to detestable sinners; it's just referring to normal people. Again, this was obviously a problem for some people in Jesus' time, but it is a problem for just about everybody in the modern age. Like everything else we've learned here, the answer is to be mindful of this kind of soil and never stop addressing it.

As Christians, cutting away the thorns that seek to choke out the fruitfulness of believers is a constant, never-ending task. Even so, we tend to forget this fact, which can leave us disgruntled, disillusioned, or even angry at the people we are trying to serve. This reveals that our expectations may not be scripturally aligned and thus may not be reasonable. It is reasonable to assume that the people in our church will struggle with seeds among thorns— with the cares of this world. And if we are honest, pastors are choking too. Family dynamics, church dynamics, cultural pressures, comparison, pressure to see results, and many other factors contribute to our own choke. But God wants us in community too so we can find freedom.

People must be constantly reminded that Christ is first— which is the foundation of the gospel itself. Christ is first as the Creator, which means all that we strive to accomplish within his creation should fall into second place in priority and emotional commitment. I'm not saying our lives are not important, but rather that Christ is our life, so therefore all of our striving to make life work apart from him is counterintuitive to the actual nature of life itself. It's like saying you don't have time to breathe—you are only fooling yourself and also likely making the process of breathing much more difficult than it should be.

When we live in community, we keep making disciples of one another by continually encouraging and reminding one another of these things—that no matter how stressed, busy, or overwhelmed we feel today, none of the cares of the world are overwhelming the life we have in Christ. It is still there, like breath in our lungs—and if we are struggling to "catch this breath" today (that is, we're responding in anger, control, fear, desperation, scheming, and the like), then the greatest gift we can receive is to have our friends tend to our soil by reminding us of the real nature of things: that Christ is first, so we don't have to carry the pressure of the number one spot today.

Who among us doesn't want fewer thorns? Life feels better when a thorn is removed, so we should foster the kind of kingdom culture in our churches where it's normal for believers to cut away thorns from each other's lives. If our culture contains a "how dare you get all up in my business" sort of attitude, we will miss some of the most helpful, fruitful, pain-relieving parts of the gospel. If our culture contains an "I won't say anything because it's none of my business" mentality, we are neglecting a major component of who Christ is actually calling us to be for others. I'm not referring to becoming a busybody or a nosy do-gooder who gossips in the name of prayer requests. I'm talking about an authentic Christianity that cares for one another, holds each other accountable, and disciples one another. Thorns don't remove themselves, and even though these thorns may have tough roots, the right kind of community pressure will always win at pulling them out because life is simply better and less painful without thorns.

We all face the cares of this world, so we need to hear again Paul's reminder to the Ephesians: "There is . . . one God and Father of all, who is over all and through all and in all."[5] Saint Patrick echoed similar sentiments that help us cut away the thorns and return to a kingdom mindset, which also happens to relieve the stresses piled on by the cares of this world. He prayed:

> Christ with me, Christ before me, Christ behind me,
> Christ in me, Christ beneath me, Christ above me,
> Christ on my right, Christ on my left,
> Christ where I lie, Christ where I sit, Christ where I arise,
> Christ in the heart of every man who thinks of me,
> Christ in the mouth of every man who speaks of me,
> Christ in every eye that sees me,
> Christ in every ear that hears me.[6]

For the modern evangelical, such wording may sound repetitious, but this perception just further reveals the way our hearts are weighed down by the cares of this world, which is why we tend to want to focus only on "bottom line" style Christianity. Make it short and sweet. Give me the basics, and tell me what I should do. Three songs, a decent sermon, and let's get on our way back to "real" life. But Saint Patrick was praying in such a way that his earthly life—what we often call "real life"—would be conformed to his actual real life in Christ.

We try to pattern our church culture after such language and practices, not assuming that anything related to Christ can be filed away in the "got it" section. We assume that the working of God's Spirit through his Word and within the community in which we live is something that is "getting us" closer to the image of Christ every day. We know that while we are busy working on whatever it is we work on, the most important work is that which God is doing in us, which is why Paul said, "It is God who works in you, both to will and to work for his good pleasure."[7] Healthy churches should be intentional about using kingdom of God language, not just as ritual or as a way to sound pious or holy, but rather just the opposite—as a means of aligning our everyday lives with the life of Christ. In other words, his words should become second nature, which is to say, first priority.

Another key verse for establishing just such a culture is found in Philippians 1:27: "[No matter what happens] only let your manner of life be worthy of the gospel of Christ." I call it my "tattoo verse" because I always joke that I'll get it tattooed on my body someday (but my wife says my lower back is already perfect just the way it is).

This has become a T-shirt verse for us, and it hangs in my office in a special spot. From an errant, works-based, earning-the-Father's-approval perspective, it can lead to insecurity—to try to become worthy of something we will never be worthy of. But that's not at all the context. It is an invitation to live in the kind of community we've been describing, where we stand firm in the same spirit with a single-minded effort to continually encourage, to sharpen, and ultimately to pull out the weeds, stones, and thorns that threaten the fruitfulness of each of us.

This is the real work of the church, so the more we build our culture on it through reminding one another from God's Word, the more we will experience the single-minded transformation that the world only dreams of—and that the cares of this world cannot choke.

Everything we do as a church should have an element of preparing the dirt in the hearts of people. It's the reason we post what we post online. It's the reason we greet you and walk you in from the guest parking lot, open the doors for you, talk to you in the lobby, show you to your seat, treat you with respect, love you no matter how you came in or who you came with, celebrate lives being changed, tell stories of how generosity is making a difference in the lives of people, preach with humor and deep conviction, sing and worship with passion and excellence, love your kids and your students, feed a lot of people, provide hundreds of thousands of volunteer hours per year, and do many tangible things to make someone's experience special.

We believe that every person who walks into our gatherings is one of four soil types. Every one of us has a prophetic responsibility to discern what sort of heart they have and turn the dirt, remove the rocks, pull the weeds, water the ground, and do whatever it takes to get their hearts ready to hear, receive, and allow the implanting of the seeds of the word of the kingdom into the turned-over, good soil of their hearts. And the promise of Jesus is that the seeds will bear fruit over and over again.

MAXIMIZE YOUR DIRT

As we near the end of our time in this particular parable, we can be encouraged to know that there is one more kind of soil—the good soil. Sure, some of the seeds fell on soil that was already in this state, which is incredible when it happens. These will be the people who are ready to help tend to the soil of others out of the gate, and I pray that God sends you people with this kind of heart soil often.

But we can learn from this part of the story that when the heart is in the right condition, the seeds grow and produce fruit on an exponential level, even reproducing new seeds and fruit from the existing fruit. So as a church, we humbly strive to be strategic in becoming and remaining a "good soil" kind of place. We keep our weeds pruned. We keep digging up our stones. We cut away each other's thorns. We keep taking sledgehammers to the hard ground. We have to keep learning to do the right kind of work. Why does this matter? Because only the culture of the kingdom rightly prepares the soil. Anything else spoils it. If we try to focus on our gifts as leaders, our abilities, our talents among the staff, or anything else, we are simply adding thorns—cares of this world—to the gospel, choking out its effectiveness in the lives of the people who show up. They may stay and may even grow, but they will struggle to be fruitful in the ways Scripture says God intends them to be.

Culture is key here, and leaders are the ones who align culture with something—either the *cares* of this world or the *culture* of the kingdom of God.

We must remember that even though it's not ideal, many people will only give you one day—Sunday—to begin building them as a disciple. It shouldn't be that way, but it will be your one shot to get them started as disciples. It cannot sustain them forever, which is why the mature, fruitful disciples will begin living this kind of life in community all seven days of the week. Nevertheless, Sundays are a big day to either perpetuate the culture of the kingdom of God or overshadow it with other things. And again, all other things—even if they have Jesus as their stated theme—will make the soil rocky, thorny, and hard.

So preach the Bible. Don't just preach pop culture. Don't just preach trendy or buzzworthy tweetables. While you can and certainly should cover topics related to modern life, rest assured that preaching verse by verse through the Scriptures is the best way to equip people for what they are facing. After all, the word of God is living and active,[8] so it never becomes outdated. Preach the hope of Christ by using the words of Christ.

Model for everyone in the churches that meet in your community, as well as everyone who may sit in the church you lead on Sunday, what Christ is actually doing in you. You have to be willing to talk about your own hard places, stony places, and thorny places. Since it is Christ who transforms a heart, you are off the hook for needing to come across as perfect—if they don't see a person who is imperfect being rescued by a Savior, how are they ever supposed to feel the need and the invitation to come home to a Savior themselves?

You are Exhibit A, and so am I. Our lives are not only on display, but they are also the proving ground for God to do great work. I've had the Lord work in me to break up the hard-hearted ground of unforgiveness toward others. He has taken me on a humility journey, using my overseers and my pastor to speak directives into my life that have called out my workaholism and the idolatry of performance and notoriety. God has deepened my devotion by calling me back to longer seasons of fasting and trusting in his plan, removing the stones of my own shallow faith at times. These may be merely anecdotal, but as the one telling the story, I'm grateful to be very much a work in progress in God's family.

As leaders, but even more as Christians, we must avoid the temptation in the American church to simply behave as overly articulate eye candy for some ultra-filtered Christianese Instagram account. Let people see the work of Christ *in you*, and you will be laying the foundations of a healthy soil culture *in them*. Be full of grace, full of truth, and then fully call people to the joy of repentance—that is, the unmistakably transformative experience of being graciously wrecked and then remade by a God who loves them enough to heal their wounds and rescue them from the cares of this world that weigh them down with fear, anxiety, and hopelessness.

Don't be content to let them be content with half-hearted, heavy lives—and certainly don't let them call such a life the full life of a disciple of Christ. Lift the weight from their shoulders with the true gospel, fully and clearly expressed in authentic community—because *that's* what the gospel seeds in the right soil do.

At our church, we tell people that our mission is to lead people to become fully devoted followers of Christ. That includes all people. So whether you're a nonbeliever, new believer, or seasoned believer, we think you (*all* of us) have room to grow—which means this is the language we should be using every week, calling everyone to nothing less than God's best intentions for their lives. We want lost people saved, saved people discipled, discipled people trained, and trained people serving Christ and others as they joyfully pursue fuller devotion today.

The idea is to engage and reengage everyone—from mature disciples to skeptical outsiders—every time we're together, and a lot more often throughout the week in community. We want to help make room for everyone to move in, no matter where they are—that's the work of soil management . . . or digging in the dirt and then doing it over and over again.

Sure, we could spend money on the best speakers, the best pastors, and the best leaders, but the truth is, they should all be preaching the same gospel—sowing the same seeds. They may not do it the same way or possess the same eloquence, education, or ministry pedigree (whatever that is), but the word of God won't fail. What our churches really need are pastors, leaders, members who are willing to do the hard work of dirt management—or soil transformation.

Historically, the people who have most transformed the agriculture industry on a mass scale are those who figured out how to maximize the dirt. Take something as familiar as the weed-killing product, Roundup. It does not produce more seeds.

It does not produce better landscapers, homeowners, or farmers. It hasn't made ears of corn produce more kernels, farmers more extroverted, or tractor drivers do a better job of pushing around the dirt. Roundup simply makes the dirt better suited for the desired outcome. And as we lead and serve the people God is bringing, we are engaging every person at the level of their heart.

We *want* to encounter people whose hearts are as hard as concrete, but seeing the seeds actually take root in their hearts takes a lot of effort. To that end, we have all four of the heart types in our church—and in our lives—every week. There are hard-hearted people who have been dragged to church by parents, spouses, grandmothers, guests, and friends. Next to them are people ready for an exchange with God and an encounter with his people—just desperate for their lives to be changed. Good soil and hard soil in the same field.

We also encounter people who are surrounded and consumed by the difficulties and cares of this world, either crowding out their life beneath or choking out their fruitfulness above. We shouldn't spend all of our efforts packaging and repackaging the seeds we've been given or making sure we secure the most sought-after new hires to throw the seeds better. Everything we do as a church is about pulling out those weeds, clearing the stones, and turning the dirt in the hearts of people.

Where are you today? Maybe as a leader, you are caught up in the thorns of image, comparison, insecurity, or laziness. Maybe you've overcomplicated the seeds and underworked the field.

Maybe you're reading this book as a favor to a friend, but your heart feels as hard as concrete. Like Blane, you're no idiot, and you've gathered some strong evidence about the nature of God and his people—and you want nothing to do with either. Maybe you're so beaten down by difficulty that the root is just not holding steady and you think you will soon wither away.

Those are a lot of maybes, but let me offer a certainty: you don't have to worry about producing life in your own heart or in the hearts of others. You can't do it anyway, so you can put down that weight and join me in a journey of looking at the only thing you have a role in—the condition of hearts, the making of room for something new to be heard and to take root. No matter how hard your ground may be—or the ground of the people you love—the seeds work.

Culture is the big result of many small decisions. Pastors, leaders, and members alike must come to the place where they decide once and for all who God has called his church to be—and lead accordingly. Scripture says that the gates of hell will not prevail against the church.[9] However, if we don't make room for the ways and the ones the Father desires, then the church is prevailing against herself. Everything we do in our churches has the potential either to prepare and cultivate good soil or to ruin the soil, sowing counterfeit seeds and hardening the soil even more. This is why it's important for the culture of our churches to always remain warm and kind yet also clear and intentional— which, contrary to popular belief, are qualities not mutually exclusive to the biblical truth lived out in true community.

PART 3

THE PARABLE OF THE TALENTS

CHAPTER 8

IT'S ALL HIS

When It's All Over, It's All His

As we move into the book's last major section, I'd like to share a bit of my own story at LifePoint Church. My purpose is not to demonstrate some sort of rags-to-riches fairy tale, the kind that so many pastors in this country dream of. Yes, if you walked into our building now and saw the thousands of people sitting there, it may create the wrong reactions. Jealousy. Insecurity. Coveting. Or maybe you have twenty thousand people in your church, and what we do looks like amateur hour to you, which would also produce the wrong reactions. Pride. Judgment. Superiority. It's a vicious cycle, isn't it?

When it comes to the church world, everyone seems to have their own minimal expectations, personal standards, and dreams—and most of us live week to week somewhere in between. I hope the pages leading up to this chapter have altered your expectation, standard, and dream just a bit, to the extent that the wrong reactions can begin to give way to kingdom reactions instead. Trust me, I haven't always had (and don't always have) the right kingdom reactions when it comes to church, especially when it comes to the comparison game many pastors and leaders feel compelled to play.

Probably as it is in your town, dozens upon dozens of churches are located within a five-mile radius of our church. So the comparison game in the community comes naturally, if nothing else by virtue of the abundance of choices. Comparison comes in many forms. No matter what our Sundays look or feel like, a simple trip into the vast world of social media reminds me that I'm not as trendy as a certain pastor or that our crowd looks different from another church's crowd.

As I mentioned earlier, LifePoint Church was recognized nationally because of the fast growth. We're deeply grateful for this, but it does mean this kind of recognition required an analysis of data and also a comparison of that data among churches. The act of comparison is not sinful in and of itself and can be helpful from an observational and evaluation standpoint. Much wisdom and insight can be harvested from that data.

But it's hard not to feel the tension that comparison creates, especially if you feel that your church is not the size you hoped for—or maybe not even growing at all. It can create feelings of frustration, isolation, and resentment toward those who are experiencing a growth curve that is different from yours. Or it can send you on the wrong kind of growth crusade—the one where you become obsessed with the numbers, taking in every book, blog, podcast, and social media post you can about how to add more butts into the seats.

The tension is real, so it may be helpful to address some of my real story. The church that is now LifePoint Church started about five years before we moved to town to take the job. The founding pastor and his team had procured land and constructed a building. At first, things went well as the church grew to about 250 attenders in five years.

After four years, the church opened a brand-new building, and a few months later, the church endured a painful leadership transition that left them without a leader for almost nine months. A couple of rounds of people leaving ensued, which dropped the church attendance to an average of fifty people or so—and on some Sundays, it was as low as twenty or thirty people. Picture it: fewer than fifty people in a beautiful, brand-new building that also happened to carry with it about $2.4 million in debt. They couldn't afford to pay their existing bills, much less pay someone to be their new pastor.

They interviewed multiple candidates, but none of them worked out. At one point, they thought they had their new pastor, voting him in unanimously. Even so, this pastor felt that God didn't want him there, so he turned it down. The church felt deeply wounded, as if they couldn't catch a break.

Around the same time, Stephanie and I were still living in Missouri but feeling a desire to come back home to Tennessee. We were part of a denominational fellowship, so I began making some calls to inquire about opportunities. None of the places we heard about seemed like places God was directing us. Then someone mentioned Clarksville, but he said it was not a church where he would send his friend.

On paper, I suppose he had a point. At the time, Clarksville was a town I was vaguely familiar with as a place I had stopped for gas or to grab a meal while driving from Knoxville to Missouri during my seminary days. I knew little to nothing about its population, demographic makeup, or church activity. I knew it had a medium-sized university (Austin Peay State University—Go, Govs!) and was a military town. I remembered it had a lot of activity around one of its exits on Interstate 24 (Exit 4—the mall exit). What stats I heard about the church there were bleak, and pretty much all of the friends or ministry leaders I told about the opportunity thought I should just keep looking.

But I had a feeling I can't fully explain. I was immediately moved by this place. I knew after my first phone call with Pastor George LeFevre, the man leading the search process, that Stephanie and I were headed there. I immediately felt a real peace, and I sensed that this church would be a big part of God's gift to Clarksville and to me. I knew he wanted to bless many families, including my own, through the work he would do here. My heart desired to take on the challenge of being the lead pastor, even though on paper, it was *not* a church I would have recommended to anyone else to take on. But as a Spirit-led people, we aren't led by papers; we are led by God.

This church and this city just made sense to me. I'm a fixer at heart. I love a challenge. I love leadership. I love the church. As an extrovert, I'm good with people, and I believe in God's plan to see people become more of who God has called them to be. Plus, you could say I'm a little stubborn. (You would be wrong—I'm *extremely* stubborn.) All this to say that there was that thing inside me that wanted to prove the naysayers wrong, even if most of those naysayers weren't necessarily real (sometimes you can be your own worst critic).

Regardless, this town is now my home. I've lived in this city longer than any other city in my life. My roots are dug in; my kids are from here; and my prayer is that God will give me an entire career here.

But in the beginning, I simply sensed that God was in this process, so I wanted to be in it too.

THE STEEP INVESTMENT

My first month on the job removed any rose-colored glasses I might have been tempted to put on before my arrival. The vote to elect me was carried out by fifty-two people. Fifty said yes. Four weeks later, I was installed as the pastor. I had very few clues as to what I was doing. I had never done this before, and it wasn't like taking on a new position on staff where they onboard you to the team, tell you all about your responsibilities, and help you commit to stay in your own lane.

I was the onboarder now; it was all "my lane."

I was given the real keys to the whole place, and all the names on the roster were now under my pastoral care. I didn't know any of them. In my first week, each vendor got a call that let them know I was the new pastor and that all of the bills were now my responsibility. I remember the feeling being similar to the moment I got my driver's license at the age of sixteen and bought my first car, only infinitely bigger.

We called the bank that first week to let them know that my name would be on the mortgage as the CEO of the corporation—a corporation that owed them $2.4 million. That's a lot of debt for a church that hadn't had one hundred people in attendance in months. My first Sunday was the last Sunday of June 2010, and as the month ended, the tithes and offerings came in $15,000 under budget for that month alone.

The board that interviewed me offered me a generous salary and benefit package, but there was no way in the world the church was going to be able to pay it consistently. We couldn't pay the mortgage or the utility bills. We didn't even have enough money to buy Goldfish crackers for the kids room at church, so there was no way the church was going to pay me. And while I appreciated the offer, I was planning on eating a lot of rice and beans—and possibly delivering pizzas again—to make ends meet. We weren't coming for the money; we were coming because God had given us this opportunity.

Because of this, God produced miracles even before we officially started. I had been elected to the position and was in the process of getting everything in order to move to Clarksville for good. Again, the people there were kind; the building was new; my wife and I were elated. But the money was bad—really bad. But God assigned us here, and where God directs us, he provides for us.

So between the Sunday I was elected and the Sunday I started, the organization that was directly next door to the church building called and offered to pay cash for four of our twenty-eight acres of property. Pastor George called me in Missouri to get my opinion and to offer to wait until my arrival to call my first board meeting to vote on selling the property. I told him not to wait but to recognize that God's hand was providing for us—and to sell it quickly! If it weren't for the sale of that land, the church could not have survived those early months. God provided in a miraculous way.

The sale of those four acres allowed us to pay the bank a chunk of cash to get on their good side again, to set aside some margins to cover the monthly deficits, and to set aside my entire first year of salary in an escrow account, which meant they could truly promise to pay me for one year. After that time, I would be on my own and become bi-vocational. Basically, God provided one year to get this going.

But it was still the early days. My first Sunday, eighty-five people showed up, including kids. The giving was low. The morale was a mix between excitement and skepticism about the new guy, and while we had a ton of vision and hope for this church, we had a long way to go to get there—or anywhere. While we faced the practical challenges of leading a church, we also faced the pastoral challenges of caring for people, loving them well, and walking many people through healing from the past year of some really painful moments. But those people were the reason we came, so that's what we did.

We began to imagine a new church—a church with a kingdom of God perspective, a church that was healthy and whole and was reaching our city well. It was a different direction from where things were when we started, and it was really, really hard. But it was also the most exciting time in my Christian life. (If you ever catch me in person and want to see me get emotional and nostalgic, ask me about those early days. I could talk about them for hours.) God is a promise maker and a promise keeper! He has been profoundly good to us every step of the way, but those early days and years were incredibly special.

Lest I digress, I'll just say the early days were both amazing and hard—and they built my faith in God like no other season of my life. They sharpened me more quickly than any training I had ever undergone. I hope you've also lost any rose-colored glasses of life in a large church. Things did not look like they do now from a facility, staff, or financial standpoint, but God was no less present, and I was no less fulfilled then with God and his people as I am now. In fact, trusting God with those issues back then seemed a lot more exciting and often easier than trusting God with the issues we face today—the stakes sometimes feel so much higher when it comes to today's issues.

Here's the thing about stewardship. It is a principle unrelated to the size, scope, or success of what has been given to you. The size of your faithfulness is what really matters. So saith the motivational ministry memes and bumper stickers sold at ministry retreats and conferences where pastors show up to get much-needed encouragement. But come on, deep down inside, we really don't believe this, do we? And much like the true reactions of our hearts to the early statements I made in the first few chapters about who builds the church (God, not us), our knee-jerk reaction to this statement also reveals a lot about what we *really* believe about church as it relates to faithfulness, stewardship, and the ways of God in dispensing opportunity, as well as in measuring our success with what he has dispensed.

So once again, Jesus has prepared a tailor-made glimpse into his higher, heavenly, and healthier perspective through the parables. His goal was to help listeners understand the culture by which he himself lives and by which he will evaluate the things we do or don't do on earth. Even so, we often still choose to measure our earthly success, especially as it relates to church work, by a different rubric. We move forward in either pride or insecurity, which indicates that we really don't understand the heart of the Father in this area of his kingdom.

In many cases, leaders and teachers have taken the principles in Scripture and twisted them around the tree of modern humanism, stripping the Scriptures of their divine intention in order to recalibrate them toward an earthly aim. They use spiritual terms to frame what are ultimately fleshly pursuits. We see this in the skewed belief that pastors of large churches have "more anointing" than pastors of small churches, as well as greater influence with God or a higher dose of his magical pixie dust of favor. People begin treating men and women of God who seem to operate on a higher plane of earthly success as greater than everyday disciples, something that any true disciple should immediately reject in deference to the humility and selflessness that accompany authentic discipleship—the kind of attitude that Jesus himself displayed. There's no room for personal kingdom building within Christ's kingdom.

If we examine the heart of Jesus in the parable of the talents, I believe we can immediately begin to experience the transformation of our attitudes and expectations toward church and our work within it as we understand and pursue God's best intentions for it.

Few biblical stories are as misunderstood as this one, often fostering in the mind of the modern reader a sense of unfairness. After all, each character in the story doesn't seem to be given equal opportunity. I would love to jump into Jesus' story and offer a few observations that may surprise you—and hopefully will encourage you to see what I think Jesus really means by this story.

"For it will be like a man going on a journey, who called his servants and entrusted to them his property. To one he gave five talents, to another two, to another one, to each according to his ability. Then he went away. He who had received the five talents went at once and traded with them, and he made five talents more. So also he who had the two talents made two talents more. But he who had received the one talent went and dug in the ground and hid his master's money. Now after a long time the master of those servants came and settled accounts with them. And he who had received the five talents came forward, bringing five talents more, saying, 'Master, you delivered to me five talents; here, I have made five talents more.' His master said to him, 'Well done, good and faithful servant. You have been faithful over a little; I will set you over much. Enter into the joy of your master.' And he also who had the two talents came forward, saying, 'Master, you delivered to me two talents; here, I have made two talents more.' His master said to him, 'Well done, good and faithful servant. You have been faithful over a little; I will set you over much. Enter into the joy of your master.' He also who had received the one talent came forward, saying, 'Master, I knew you to be a hard man, reaping where you did not sow, and gathering where you scattered no seed, so I was afraid, and I went and hid your talent in the ground. Here, you have what is yours.' But his master answered him, 'You wicked and slothful servant! You knew that I reap where

I have not sown and gather where I scattered no seed? Then
you ought to have invested my money with the bankers, and
at my coming I should have received what was my own with
interest. So take the talent from him and give it to him who
has the ten talents. For to everyone who has will more be
given, and he will have an abundance. But from the one
who has not, even what he has will be taken away.'"

Matthew 25:14–29

The parable starts out with a landowner (who represents God
in this parable) who left his estate to go on an extended trip. We're
not told where he went or for how long—all we know is that at least
a portion of his estate, along with all the daily work it entailed,
was entrusted into the hands of three of his servants (meant to
represent us in this parable) for the duration of his journey abroad.

Now the matter of "how much" came into play, which in
our culture of quantification as the basis for measuring success is
where we tend to get hung up in this story. Show me the money!
And the landowner did—in an incredible way. To the first servant, he gave five talents. We obviously don't have a currency
nowadays called a talent, so it will be helpful to understand what
this meant—and in doing so, I think you'll be shocked to discover
the scope of this interchange between the master and the servants.

The ESV footnote for Matthew 25:15 reveals that a talent
was a financial measurement equivalent to about twenty years'
worth of income. Chew on that for a moment. One talent was
worth two decades of a laborer's annual salary. No matter what
your income, that much money at one time would be amazing.
Let's run the numbers for an average wage-earning family in
America. A simple internet search offers a ballpark estimate
of the 2018 average median household income in the United
States, which was $63,179.[1] Let's round down to $60,000, just to

simplify. This means the modern equivalent of an ancient talent (twenty years' wages) would be roughly $1.2 million.[2]

The math makes this parable more amazing. This first servant, having received five talents from the master, or one hundred years' worth of income, received somewhere in the neighborhood of $6 million. Now I don't know what you make, but in my town, that's a lot of money. If we continue these kinds of mathematical deductions for the other servants, we find that the second servant received quite a bit less, a mere $2.4 million in today's economy, while the modern martyr who has become the focal point of this story, the third servant, was given only $1.2 million. Don't forget, it was money that none of them had to earn but had been freely given by the master. More on that soon.

We will address our issues with these comparisons in the next chapter, but it's important to acknowledge them here—and to admit that every one of us reading this book would be more than happy to stumble onto any three of these financial situations, both personally and organizationally. No debt and, at minimum, about $1.5 million in the bank as an operational budget? Yeah, sign me up for that. Oh, and all we have to do is use it to do good for the master? I'm in.

But let's be real, most people who insert themselves into the details of this story struggle with the disproportionate distribution of the wealth among the various servants. Again, we'll discuss the master's reason in the next chapter, but the *what* here is probably just as important as the *why*. A lot of leaders feel they must be a one-talent servant, someone to whom God has entrusted only a little—by which we mean money, abilities, opportunities, or numbers of people.

The reality is that even the one-talent servant was made rich by the generous investment of the master—and so are we. No matter what God has entrusted to us, it's his and we are incredibly well supplied because our Master backs his investment in us. Our insecure way of looking at ministry through the lenses of martyrdom and scarcity reveals how little we understand "the unsearchable riches of Christ"[3] or "the riches of his glorious inheritance in the saints."[4] Pay attention to these words—the riches are actually found *in* the saints—in the people of God living in community together beneath the transformative grace and truth of the gospel. We often walk around groaning like ministerial paupers, but this story reveals that even the least of the servants of this particular master had access to nearly limitless resources.

This is the beginning of understanding true stewardship: *It's all God's*, and when we reside in him by faith in Christ, access is granted to us for purposes that align with the culture of his kingdom. We must stop waiting for more people to show up, more offerings to be given, more land to sell, more investments to pay off, more web pages to be updated, more videos to be made, more of the "right" people to move into the neighborhoods near our churches, or more notoriety to come our way because of our ability to preach or lead. All we have, God has given us. We aren't leading with our own resources; we are using the resources of the Master for the purposes of the Master.

The journey to sound stewardship of our lives and ministries begins by realizing just how rich our Master is, not just in resources, but also in love and entrustment of these resources to us his servants.

WHAT WE GET AND WHAT WE KEEP

Understanding the principles of what it means to truly work for kingdom purposes using the King's resources requires that, once and for all, we realize a central truth: what we have is not ours. The master in the story did not give his servants talents to keep for themselves. Rather, he entrusted to them talents with the expectation that he would come back to collect all the gains. Even so, they could freely use these talents for purposes they knew would honor the master.

We often lose our way here, even if only subconsciously or emotionally. We live our lives in ministry as if we've been entrusted with something, but deep inside, we still think it's ours—but it's not. As this story reveals from its very beginning, it's all God's.

Have you ever borrowed someone else's car? Did you treat it differently than your own car, paying more attention to the speed limit, taking your empty Starbucks cups out of the cup holder, and making sure the gas tank was full? Why do you do this? The answer is simple. Because you have to give the car back to its owner. You treat the car differently because you know it's not yours, and the car's condition upon its return reflects the level of your respect, honor, and gratitude for your friend. And certainly you would never dream of keeping the car with no explanation, locking it away in your garage, refusing to answer your friend's text asking about it, and then eventually trying to get it titled in your name.

No, you expect the owner to show up and retake possession of what is rightfully theirs. That's what happened in Jesus' parable as well. One day, after a long time of being away, the landowner returned to settle accounts. He came back to get his stuff. This will happen to us someday as well—Jesus will return, and we will have an interaction with him regarding the work we have done with what he has entrusted to us.

I think many people freak out about this concept—like a biblical showdown in which we will all pay the piper. Yes, there will be a judgment day, but note the tone of this meeting between the master and his servants. It is not harsh. The master isn't accompanied by armed bodyguards. It's just the logical process that should follow the outpouring of such grace—that is, what they should have expected and anticipated with joy. He entrusted to them treasure beyond their wildest dreams, to do what they had always dreamed of doing. Imagine what you could do in real estate, in the stock market, or in starting a business if someone were to hand you startup capital of $1 to $2 million. Even just placing this kind of cash in a basic bank account—much less a mutual fund or a more aggressive investment strategy—would yield some significant returns. (This concept will play into the story later.)

These servants should have been more than thrilled to see their master return because they already fully knew his gracious, generous nature. He had already proven it to them a million times over and more, providing for their daily needs as his servants living on his estate and entrusting into their care many fortunes. This indicated they were highly valued by the master. He had set them up for almost certain success, which was his intention.

Those who should fear a day of judgment are those who have openly refused to be servants of the Master at all. Any of us who are servants should realize God's intention and his provision—we are already loaded with his grace capital, possessing as trusted servants within his kingdom nothing less than many fortunes.

And yet we often live and lead as if there is no hope because of all that we lack in ministry—and yes, this can be money, but I'm speaking more of the general "playing the lottery" feeling many church leaders have regarding their influence, abilities, and general rapport that lead to explosive growth.

Belief is the key here—and not in some prosperity gospel sort of way. This is not about Cadillacs and corner church offices.

I'm talking about the purposes of the master's estate as it was revealed in the father's heart on the farm in the parable of the two sons to the seeds' effective work in all kinds of hearts in the parable of the sower, which is why we work to make room for every child and in every type of soil. This is about God's plan from the beginning of time to redeem his children and restore them to all that he desires for them, not about our popularity or success in ministry as it is so often measured, even if only within the secret chambers of the leader's heart.

But for God's true mission, the resources we need come from him—and they are abundant and available now. Every resource you currently have has been given to you by God.

We may be broken people, but we've already been granted divine completion for these purposes—because God is with us and promises to remain with us: "For in Him all the fullness of Deity dwells in bodily form, and in Him *you have been made complete*, and He is the head over all rule and authority."[5] Furthermore, "his divine power has *granted to us all things that pertain to life and godliness*, through the knowledge of him who called us to his own glory and excellence."[6]

As I said, belief is key here—so do we really believe these Scripture verses? Do we really believe that, in Christ, we are complete and have been granted all the things we need to be successful in being and making disciples—that is, in being *the* church? Turning or returning to this belief is the only solid basis for sound stewardship, especially as it pertains to our work as disciples and within his church.

These three beloved servants had their moment of settling accounts with their beloved master, just as we will. And it was mostly a joyful experience, as it should be. The first servant had worked hard and doubled the master's investment—and the master called him "good and faithful." Nice. The same thing happened with the second servant. But if we pause here, we encounter a fascinating observation. The master told both of these servants, "You have been faithful *over a little*; I will set you over much. Enter into the joy of your master."[7] What? He had been faithful over *a little*? These two guys had been collectively entrusted with roughly $8 million of investment capital! This reminds us that no matter our scope of leadership, ministry, or influence, whether our platform is like that of Billy Graham, Bishop Jakes, Pastor Chris Hodges, or a no-name like Mike Burnette, it's all small in God's economy. He has entrusted us with "a little" part of his vast and timeless kingdom.

We freak out over numbers—butts, buildings, and budgets—so Jesus helps us see just how small everything most easily measurable in earthly terms truly is in relation to his kingdom, which is eternal and immeasurable. No matter how big or small you may seem to be here, you're just a blip on the historical kingdom radar screen—a short footnote in tiny font barely visible on the ecclesiastical calendar. In the grand scheme of church work, Graham, Jakes, Hodges, myself, you, and a bunch of other people whose names we will never know each have about a thirty- or forty-year span to work with what has been entrusted to us. We're part of the same church as the apostles—Paul, Peter, James, John, and you can add your name to the ever-growing list—working with the same talents given by the same Master. Breathe easy; it's all his.

All of these Bible characters were heroes of the faith who lived and led well, and they all died. They all met up with the Master to settle accounts for what they did with his stuff. They were all loved well by the Master and entrusted with capital in his kingdom with which to conduct the kingdom business of making room for prodigals to come home and for turning over the soil of hearts so the seeds could take root in them. Their Master and their mission are the same as mine—the same as yours. Comprehending your place in the big picture is the beginning of good stewardship because it leads you away from a self-centered ministry that builds edifices to your own self because it appears that you have a whopping five talents, which, again, are not even yours and are minuscule in the economy of the Master.

In fact, some people get caught up in this story and think that the master allowed the servants to keep what they had invested and earned, as if these earnings were somehow their rewards. But this isn't at all what the parable reveals. They did not receive any commission or any monetary rewards. There was no 3 percent, 5 percent, or 10 percent cut of the action. What they did receive was a greater degree of entrusting—more talents for more labor in the kingdom. In other words, their faithfulness in the work they had been given produced more work for them to do *for the master,* work in which their proven faithfulness would be required. More work and more talents, which will also be settled up later and turned back in.

But in terms of rewards, theirs was much more valuable than the investment capital they had been given or would be given in their future. Their reward was to "enter into the joy of your master." In other words, they received affirmation from the master, followed by an ongoing relationship with him—and *that* was worth more than a million lifetimes of talents. "Great job! Come hang with me forever!" That is the reward!

But in terms of the money, they handed it all back to the one to whom it belonged—and we will do the same. The work I do in the Lord's kingdom is with the Lord's capital, and one day I'm going to turn it all back in: the building, the position, and, most importantly, the people—God's people. Someday I will hand over the keys of my office to the next guy. I will turn it all back in one day for a good reason: none of it is mine!

Nothing we do in ministry (or in life, actually) is about ownership; it's about management. How well are we stewarding what has been entrusted to us? And by the way, we're not just stewarding *stuff*; we're stewarding *souls*. It's about people, but so many of us get stuck in the rut of stewarding mortgages, copy paper, meetings, carpeting, reputations, and the like. These are just tools to be used and managed well, but what we prioritize to steward before the Father is the resource of human beings. These are the only things that last forever.

These are also the only things God wants us to turn back in. Quite frankly, the way we treat everything in ministry other than people reveals a lot about what we think will define our legacies. We're not going to get to heaven someday and see a collection of church buildings; those things will not go with us. Let me say, I am so grateful for the temporal things we enjoy—buildings, land, our jobs, and the like, and all of these should be handled with care as working for God. But the only thing we will turn back in are the souls of people whom God entrusted to us, which is why the ultimate work of the church is to be and to make disciples. The talents—the vested capital of infinite worth that God entrusts into our hands as stewards—are, above all else, his people.

And with his people come all the resources your church will need. The funding, the buildings, the leaders, the staffing, and the resources are all found *within* the people he has entrusted to you. Stewarding them well will involve discipling them well so that the people of God provide for that part of the work he has stewarded to us. Realizing this truth is part of another whole teaching about trusting God's provision through the people he keeps providing. (Perhaps that will be my next book—but I should finish this one first!)

Everything that has been entrusted to us is not ours to start with, which means it's not ours to end with. We will lay claim to none of it, which is why our name shouldn't be plastered on the church marquee and why we shouldn't think of the church people as "our" people.

I touched on this briefly earlier, but let me expand a little. In speaking with and coaching pastors across the nation, "my people" is a common expression, especially when we begin to suggest that a leader make changes to their community dynamics and ethic to make them more reflective of the culture of the kingdom of God. In some cases, we've even met with pastors who are interested in merging their congregations with ours, and in many of these cases, the same expression comes up. "You know, *my* people would never go for that. *My* people don't do small groups. *My* people would never give that way, worship to those songs, watch their preacher on a screen, serve that way, or change their mindsets in that way."

I love them (and you) too much not to say something. With as much grace as I can muster, I often tell them, "Those are not *your* people." They are *God's* people, and if that sounds so specific and trite that it needn't be said, I implore you not to think of this as just a matter of semantics—this is a matter of aligning our words with the correct beliefs, both for our sakes as leaders and for the sake of those we lead. After all, most of the unhealthy churches in our nation self-identify less with the gospel and more with the talents, charisma, and appearance of "their" lead pastors.

So I'll say it one more time, because this brings such freedom: they are *God's* people. They're *his* talents, and our job is to steward them in a way that moves them toward devotion to *his* kingdom concepts—a culture of generosity, a culture of grace, a high view of the authority of God's Word, a culture of diversity, a culture of truth and transparency, community, a kingdom culture of invitation, and many other ethics we've been exploring throughout this book. We will present back to God that which is most valuable to him—his children. We won't do so as their owners, but as co-stewards with them of their discipleship.

It all gets turned back in because God is the Master—and the reward we often overlook as we seek infinitely lesser, temporal things is the eternal joy of his gracious approval and the immeasurable treasure of being invited to live in close relationship with him and his people forever.

CHAPTER 9

WHAT'S YOURS IS NOT MINE

If We Don't Have It, God Doesn't Want Us to Have It

Now that we understand the amazing truth of just how much each servant in the story was given to invest, we can deal with the elephant in the parable—the apparent disparity in the dispensing of talents. This is where most of our minds immediately go, and it certainly seems to be where many of us get bogged down in the mire of pride or insecurity or both.

The key to finding peace as good stewards regarding this part of the story is to listen to what Jesus said in the beginning of its telling: "To one he gave five talents, to another two, to another one, to each *according to his ability*. Then he went away."[1]

How did the master disperse his goods? He gave to these three guys according to *their ability*, which apparently he was able to clearly see in them. He knew them well, perhaps even better than they knew themselves. The master discerned what they could handle and gave to them accordingly. They didn't petition for more. They didn't apply for bigger or smaller talents.

They didn't argue with him about fairness or lobby for making sure each worker was given the same portion or expectation.

The five-talent guy did not break out into an insecure diatribe, saying, "Oh, I don't know if I can handle this." Neither did he puff up with pride and say, "Are you sure you don't want me to handle all eight talents?" For all of the shade we sometimes throw at the one-talent servant, he didn't question or argue with the master's decision to entrust to him twenty years' worth of pay. In fact, the one-talent servant's complaint was not that he wasn't given enough by the master. Quite the opposite. He was overwhelmed by the weight of what he had been given and the master's expectations. More on that in a moment.

The point is that each servant was given something different by the master for a reason. They did not have the same giftings or abilities. This may be offensive to the modern mind, but it must be addressed if we are to align ourselves with God's culture rather than the one that is killing the health and effectiveness of most churches and their leaders. It's hard to separate Western, democratic, egalitarian thought—or really, just basic playground rules—from the kingdom-based ethos Jesus desires to establish in each of us as his church. The ways of the kingdom are foreign concepts to our human sensibilities. God doesn't operate with the broken concepts of fairness and equity the way we do. His ways are better.

Since childhood, we've been led to filter life through fairness and equity, where there are no winners and everyone gets a trophy, at least that's been the case for the past couple of decades. While this approach may stroke our fragile egos when we're young, it crushes us when we are older because God doesn't entrust to everyone the same measure of his kingdom, which leads to competition and unhealthy comparison.

We tend to wonder—and we feel no qualms in doing so

because the concept is so ingrained in our cultural climate—
why the master thought it fair and expedient to give one servant
five talents and another two and then the third servant only one
talent. Moreover, he then seemed to get upset with the one to
whom he had given less in the first place. Something about it
feels off-putting. I think it's the playground kid in us.

Let's get to the real issue here. If you think of yourself as a
five-talent guy or gal, you probably aren't *that* offended by the
story. (Whether you're actually a five-talent person is a different
question.) But I find that most of us who read this story with a
hint of offense in our hearts do so from the vantage point of the
one-talent servant. We usually come to an unspoken conclusion
after reading a book, listening to a podcast, attending a confer-
ence, or visiting a church led by others we consider to be five-
talent material. The unspoken conclusion is that there is a sort
of spiritual caste system that develops between the haves and the
have-nots, the *has-been-given-muchs* and the plain old *has-beens*.

We've all been to those conferences, right? We sip hand-
crafted Starbucks-quality lattes in someone else's massive coffee
shop, watch videos featuring another church's blissful members
who throw themselves into every volunteer ministry in the church,
and hear someone else's tales of what it's like to live with no debt
on a massive campus worth millions of dollars. Our insecurities
and shame begin to build. We hide it and bottle up the poison
where it can do more damage within us.

Back home in our churches, we aren't sure if anyone will care
for the babies in the nursery—or if any babies will even show up.
We aren't sure there will be enough money in the offering plate
to pay this month's mortgage; we are not confident that the room
will be even half full—after all, there are so many bigger and
better options in town. This feeling never leaves the heart of a
leader. Jesus knew at his final supper that one would leave him,

and then at his final prayer in Gethsemane, he knew his best friends wouldn't show up.

In our hearts, where no one can hear us, we ask the Master, *Why did you give this other person five talents—enough to plant extra campuses in four of the surrounding towns—but you only gave me one talent so I can't even get the plant in my office to grow, the one left over from the latest funeral I had to officiate? Why do you grow that place and not my place?* These sentiments reflect the hearts of those of us who live and die in the name of fairness and comparison. Most of us have either been there before (I know I have many times), or we live there consistently in our everyday lives.

Social media compounds this problem, elevating it to an exponential, almost epidemic level. I hate Instagram on Sundays because it gives every one of us a front-row seat to everyone else's chosen images of success. I stay away from Instagram on Sundays because I see what all my buddies are doing, and while I'm pumped for them and proud of them, the playground kid in me always shows up and falls into comparison. I wish it didn't bother me, but it does. My church may or may not be bigger than theirs, but theirs look different on social media—cooler, hipper, trendier, healthier than mine. And now you can see just how quickly I can lose my way because my heart is calling it "my" church.

We can have a record attendance Sunday, but my heart becomes more worried about how it appears on social media, which leads me to feel depressed and anxious. Let me be clear, this is not an issue with any of my fellow church leaders. It's clearly an issue with me that must die as it is submitted to the kingdom of God, not the kingdom of me or the kingdom of comparison. Here's another secret: my pastor friends tell me they struggle with this at various levels too. (Thanks for your prayers for your pastors and pastor friends!)

And over what? Over comparisons with others' talents versus

what I've been given. We've been conditioned to compare our treasures and never let on about our scarcity. Let's be real—no one ever posts a filtered picture of a half-empty sanctuary with a caption that reads:

> Welp, most of them didn't show up again. We announced a baptism, but nobody signed up. Music was less than great, but whatcha gonna do when your worship leader sounds like a wounded giraffe? At least we got out in time to beat the [insert random denomination] folks to the buffet. #SoBlessed #ComeOnSomebody #AintNoPartyLike ASundayMorningParty #WhereMyPeopleAt #ForReal WhereTheyAt???

Comparison is a natural place to lose yourself, but a supernatural perspective can help you find yourself again within the context of the Master's heart, the same heart we've been talking about since the first parable. The bottom line is this: the Master doled out a lifetime of treasure to each of his servants—and again, none of it was theirs. It was an amazing expression of grace.

And so was this: the Master gave to each servant *according to his ability*. I truly believe in this concept for any person in the family of God, not just church leaders. I want to assure you, no matter what you're leading or serving, that God knows what he has given you. Whether you're a pastor of a large or small, growing or plateaued place—and that includes your family, your job, your creative pursuit, or a hundred other possibilities that include church but aren't limited to church—God knows what he's entrusted to your care. You can trust that he knows what he has given you, whether it's a part-time role at a fast-food restaurant or the CEO position. If you have a large nuclear family or are entrusted to raise multiple kids alone (as my mom did), you can trust that God knows what he is doing and what he has entrusted to you. Again, he gave to each servant according to that servant's ability—and that is good, merciful news, not a reason to feel slighted.

DEALING WITH GROWTH

If we can accept the previous sentence and get over the hurdles of fairness and comparison, I truly believe we can be set free from the trap of insecurity and begin to live as true stewards whose work will prove to be pleasing to the master when the accounts are finally settled. It all comes down to this: the master had the wisdom and wherewithal to decide what each of his servants could handle. What they will do with what he gave them was yet to be seen, but he knew what they could handle when he entrusted things to them. He knew what level of investment would be a solid foundation for their respective future successes, but he also knew what level would be too heavy—a millstone rather than a foundation stone—for each of them to bear, leading to endless failures. He knew their boundaries, their potential, and their weaknesses, so he disbursed talents to them accordingly. He did this intentionally, not haphazardly.

Yes, the master acknowledged what no one in the modern age wants to: the servants were not equal in their abilities. They were equal in value to the master, but they were not equal in disposition, leadership ability, or—yes, dare we say it—talent. (No pun intended; okay, it was a little intended.)

Before you freak out, let's be clear about what this *doesn't* mean. It *doesn't* mean all the pastors and leaders of big churches are "more talented" than all the pastors and leaders of small or medium-sized churches. Attendance seems to be the one thing we most want to compare. But even though there are so many factors other than attendance that determine our success in ministry, we must at least acknowledge that God doesn't assign us all to the same places, to the same length of stay, or to the same growth patterns or results. *Faithfulness* is our standard, not results. Every servant's experience will be different because every servant is intimately known by the Master.

Our expectations and perceptions of success must be challenged by Scripture and wholehearted devotion to God's ways. We must stop comparing talents.

After spending most of his ministry traveling from town to town, the apostle Paul wrote a letter to his protégé, Timothy, that revealed a different kind of ending from the one most of us want as leaders.[2] He was in jail, lamenting that many of his ministry colleagues—most of whom he had led to Christ himself—were no longer with him. He was mostly alone, an old guy waiting for an execution he knew would someday come, probably sooner than later, and asking for a stack of old letters or scrolls and a winter coat to keep warm in the coming cold.

One of his friends, Demas, had abandoned the faith, "in love with this present world."[3] Another guy, a nonbelieving coppersmith named Alexander, had done much harm to Paul's ministry and reputation, and seemingly nothing could be done to stop him. Another friend, Trophimus, had to be left behind because he was too ill to travel. How many miraculous healings Paul had performed, and yet this was happening to him and his friends. His words reveal so much about his reality of what it meant to follow Christ completely: "At my first defense no one came to stand by me, but all deserted me."[4]

There were no book deals. No huge sanctuaries. No coffee shops. No chance of getting out of this ministry thing without a brutal execution God told him was coming, and probably soon.

(This list would make quite the brochure for your church ministry internship, don't you think?) And yet most of us would agree that Paul was a five-talent kind of servant.

You see, the way we measure talents and growth—that is, success—does relate to the act of more people coming to know Christ; it just doesn't necessarily relate to it in a week-to-week attendance roster or according to a predictable metric of growth. No, each of us has a role in Christ's ultimate plan that is hand-crafted by the Master. He is investing in you with an expectation unrelated to the outcome, success, or efficiency of the other servants he has invested in. He only expects from you what he knows is yours to produce. I know it would be so much easier if we knew our own potential as well, but that's where faith comes in.

The parable of the talents is a story about capacity, not comparison. The master expected the same thing from each of the servants—that they would fully use what they had been given. In other words, the size of the tank of potential within them didn't matter; it only mattered that each pursued fullness. The master wasn't measuring the number of talents; he was measuring the proportion of their pursuits, just as two out of two equals 100 percent and a million out of a million also equals 100 percent. It was the 100 percent trust he was seeking from them, regardless of their capacity.

And again, no one had the same capacity. Who knows, if the parable had been longer, perhaps ten servants would have received ten different amounts to steward. Regardless, we all tend to want the same thing as the one we perceive to have the highest number of talents—except, of course, the lonely guy in prison who asked for his winter coat, who also happened to have written nearly half of the New Testament books. We want the same perceived success as someone else; we just want it in our own towns and on our own terms. But God has entrusted to you what he believes is right for you to handle, which may offend your Western sensibilities that have taught you that anyone can do anything if they just try really hard.

You are special, and your value to the Master knows no limit. You may not become everything your mom said you could be—and that's okay. You are going to be something better—the exact person to whom God knows exactly what to entrust. Remember, it's all his anyway. Why do we care how he gives it out? Be faithful with his entrustment. According to the parable, the master entrusts based on ability, not necessarily based on character. I mention this because we've all heard of broken and characterless leaders who took what God gave them and hurt others, took advantage, or misused (or even abused) their authority or influence. Why did God entrust anything to these leaders—or anything to the third servant in the parable—knowing they wouldn't steward it well?

Remember that parables and metaphors aren't meant to be inclusive of every lesson that can be learned from every imaginable scenario—this is why Jesus used so many parables instead of just one big story to cover everything. To that end, this story seems to be more about the principles of stewardship within the safety of God's sovereignty than about all of the unanswerable questions related to God's sovereignty. In theory, the master in the story (who represents God) is already a bit separated from every aspect of his divinity simply by the fact that he traveled, something that God, who is omnipresent, technically doesn't do. If you're already everywhere, how would you go on a journey to another somewhere? Again, it would appear that Jesus' point in this parable was not about the minutiae of why unfaithful servants are sometimes still entrusted with influence or resources, though this is a mystery addressed repeatedly throughout Scripture, especially in the Psalms.

Jesus seemed more concerned that each servant recognize and own what the master had entrusted to them—and he seemed uninterested in answering for the other servants why he had given what he had given to their counterparts. All of the servants in the parable proved a point: their true character was revealed in the crucible of influence. It doesn't change the fact that God entrusts us with something, but as the ending of the story reveals, it can become the reason that God won't entrust us with more.

God is looking out for you when he doesn't give you the exact seat, position, amount of influence, or skill you want because he knows whether you can handle them in a way that will honor his purposes for your life and, more importantly, for his kingdom. This isn't a question of whether or not you can sustain a larger church—God may not care much about that question, even though we are obsessed with it. I've met many pastors who only want to talk about three things: growth, growth, and explosive growth. They want it at any cost, but that is not the kind of cost we are supposed to be counting. Stewardship begins not with the desire to produce results, but with the realization that you've been given a specific investment for a specific reason, even if that reason hasn't yet been revealed. Good stewards want the exact results their master has uniquely equipped them to produce.

Can we work with what we've been given? That's the real question.

Even though I know LifePoint Church has grown more quickly than most churches, this result is a reflection of God's purposes in our town and in our team. After all, the day is coming when we will give it all back—when the keys will reside on someone else's key chain. But I can give you a few numbers that are less impressive than our current attendance, if that will help.

Eighty-five people in attendance, $2.4 million in debt, and one building covered in taupe—those were the talents God thought I could handle. It was my moment of great joy because the value of what God was entrusting to me for my short time of life and ministry on this earth was infinitely higher than these quantifiable things. God basically said to me, "You're thirty years old and only two years out of seminary. You have a chip on your shoulder, arrogance in your heart, a beautiful wife, and two beautiful little girls. I'll let you shepherd these eighty-five people of mine because they're wounded and I love them, and I know that's about all you can handle."

Those were smaller days, but they were incredible days because God knew what I could handle—and through the process of handling what I was made to handle, he finally knocked that chip off my shoulder, threw the water of humility on my internal fire of arrogance, and, above all, kept showing up to grow his church as I focused on stewarding the assignment before me. Even as I write this paragraph, I'm reminded how surprised I am by this reality and how humbling it is to see what God has done here. I don't know why God grew LifePoint Church the way he chose to, and I'm convinced that my story is not a one-size-fits-all story. Being faithful in your context won't always produce numerical growth, though it may—there are many other trustworthy elements of his stewardship that are at play, many of which are beyond our knowledge on this side of eternity.

That's why I say, as you've already heard, that we never grew *our* church. It was never *our* church in the first place, and God is the only one who produces growth. I just showed up, turned some soil, welcomed the unwelcome, and kept working hard with what I was entrusted.

I have been more surprised than anyone when God continues to tell us that he thinks we can steward more. For what it's worth, this was *way* easier before the church became big. I slept better at night. I didn't have to resolve nearly as many conflicts.

I didn't feel as much pressure. The visibility wasn't as high. Fewer divorces. Fewer funerals. Fewer pains. I love where we are, but it's a different kind of love. I *really* loved where we were, and I miss those days. I confess that I took those days for granted and kept my eye on the next hill to climb, the next service to start, the next building to build.

Yet back then and today, God knows what I can handle. He knows both the potential and the potential pitfalls of each of us—and we can rest in the truth that, no matter what size our attendance balloons up to or whittles down to, he knows what he is doing with me. He knows what he is doing with you too.

There is more to what I do than can be quantified by this one number called attendance. If it quantifies anything, it's God's work of grace in the hearts of the people in our community. We don't create it; we attempt to steward his creation in a way that will continue to create room for him to exponentially foster this life in the hearts of those he loves, which is where the highest value is found.

Our churches and our work as Christ followers are not ours; we are merely stewards of what God has given us for the time he has appointed. This attitude frees us from owning what we can't own so we can fully own what we should. Everything we have, God has entrusted to us; everything we don't have, God hasn't entrusted to us—yet. We aren't responsible for anyone else's church; we're responsible only for what God knows we can handle. Breathe.

THE HAND YOU'RE DEALT

Now that we're addressing the topic of church growth as most of us have thought about it, I can tell you that a part of the "talents" that God has aligned with our abilities will sometimes include the ability to motivate, organize, and sustain people in community. I don't want to come off as though growth is a completely and divinely random occurrence. I certainly believe it is divinely ordered and empowered, but so is the wisdom God gives to work toward it and steward it.

Nothing God does is random.

But there is the matter of working as a good steward. We should work hard, regardless of our situations or perceived abilities. I only want to help you separate all of the countable metrics from the expectation of what it means to be a good steward. We will dive into this in the next chapter when we examine the attitude of the one-talent servant.

But my guess is that the five-talent guy worked very hard. I bet he was focused, diversifying his strategies and willing to take risks that made sense for his investment goals. He probably found a niche—the one the master knew he would find and equipped him to pursue successfully. No matter how much you've been given, work as if it is all you've been given and you're doing all you can with it for your Master.

At LifePoint, we're trying to stay focused on a healthy church culture with healthy systems. We feel an obligation to steward well what the Lord has entrusted to us. And as we keep entering seasons where God entrusts us with more, the feeling of gratitude and the weight of the stewardship (the good kind of weight) feel the same as when he entrusted us with eighty-five members.

I fight against entitlement. I never want to say to myself, *Look at what I've built!* The bottom line is that God can snatch this thing away in a heartbeat—it is not mine now, and it never will be. I could die or have a moral failure (God forbid), or the Lord could wake me up in the middle of the night and call me to serve in the mission field of Hawaii. Whatever happens, his grace is my anchor, and whatever he calls me to do will be a gift of entrustment from him. He is the boss, no matter how many awards my church wins for its size or how many people like my sermons online or at a Sunday service.

This is the hand I've been dealt for now—and you've been dealt one too. The thing is, you may or may not be looking at the cards he intends for you; that is, you may not be in the right situation just yet. It may be time for a change of location, but even more, many people struggle in stewardship because they need a change of heart. Joseph didn't need a quality opportunity to be a quality servant—Potiphar's house and the Egyptian dungeon were just fine for God's desired goals to be fulfilled in his life. Betrayal by his own family, false accusation by his boss's wife, and years upon years in a prison cell he didn't deserve—yeah, just another five-talent servant.

That's why we must not look at buildings and attendance as the only measures of potential or the markers of success. Look at what's in your hands right now because I promise you that if you are the Master's servant, it is something of immense value. I've had pastors walk up to me after we hosted leadership events and say, "Well, it's easy for you to say all of this when you're in this big building with all these people and all this money." My heart breaks when they say this, especially when they can't see that we did not start there at all. They are not spiritually confined or judged by the number of people in their churches or dollars in their bank accounts. They are beloved servants who have been entrusted with something—but they may be burying it in the ground because they don't understand the heart of the Master.

The Master's heart, as we'll see in the next chapter, will lead them to understand that his chief expectation for them is found not in their *fruitfulness* but in their *faithfulness*, a truth hidden in the plain sight of religious rhetoric and assumption. Some of the greatest stories of fruitful growth are actually stories of faithfulness. Stories about great organizations and leaders—if you read between the lines and look beyond their stats—are stories about taking something at one point and being faithful with it to the next point and then the next and then the next. I can name many small and large organizations—and every size in between—that model faithfulness. I pray that each of us reading these words will endeavor to be found in their company.

CHAPTER 10

DON'T JUST GROW . . . GROW FAITHFUL

It's God's Job to Grow His Church;
It's Our Job to Grow in Faithfulness

know it's hard to believe, but we've come to the last chapter. It is my deepest and sincerest hope that something we've dialogued about in these pages has made a difference in how you see the ways of Jesus and the heart of the Father revealed in the stories Jesus told. I could have written about a hundred other takeaways from many other parables, which, I think, was the point Jesus made in using allegories and metaphors—there is always more to learn and apply, especially since Jesus' words are not static and stationary, but rather living and active.[1]

In fact, *living* and *active* are fitting terms for describing the real expectation of stewardship in the life of a disciple. For this, we turn to the most infamous of servants in the story—the one-talent guy. Remember, this is the servant most of us identify with in terms of what we've been given by the Master, yet we tend to distance ourselves from this servant in terms of what is expected of us. Perhaps we should pay extra attention to the guy who reminds us the most of ourselves, even if doing so is uncomfortable. The takeaway from his story may even surprise you and give you a little encouragement.

As the master came to this servant, I bet the servant was feeling good about the entire process. The first servant honored the master, doubled his share of resources, and had heard a "well done." The second servant honored the master, presented a 100 percent increase, and had also gotten a "well done." Perhaps he was going to be a "three for three." The first two guys addressed the master appropriately: "Master, you gave me this; here's what I did with it." The third guy started off right. As he stepped up and said, "Master . . ." I'm sure the boss was excited about what he would say next. But that's where the third servant deviated from the script, and the master was sorely disappointed (but not for the reasons we might expect).

The third servant had an explanation for his master that revealed where the real problem lay. He told his master that he saw him as a tough boss, a hard man, collecting on what he hadn't worked for—reaping where he hadn't sown and gathering where he hadn't scattered. These words revealed the servant's own heart more than they revealed anything about the master. This is an interesting mini-metaphor wrapped up in a parable wrapped up in a quandary—and it led the servant to the ultimate confusion of belief about this master.

There was the real problem: he believed wrongly about the nature of his master.

We want to focus on what this servant did—or did not do, in this case—when he buried his talent in the backyard so he could return it "as is" to his master. We fail to see why he did what he did: he didn't know his master at all. He didn't know the heart of his benevolent master. He couldn't see that his master had put a lot of trust in him to begin with. After being handed more than a million dollars of investment capital, he somehow thought the master was "a hard man" who hadn't done his part to make any real return on this money.

He couldn't see that the master had sown directly into him—and with more than he could have ever gathered on his own. He couldn't see the value of the gift because he couldn't see the heart of the master. And that, my friends, is the real crux of the matter of stewardship in ministry. Lest we forget, this man was a servant—another accurate term would be a "minister." He was not a stranger or an unbeliever. He was one who lived in the grace of the master's estate but didn't believe that the heart of the master was very gracious and good.

The result was that he squandered the treasure of another that was in his possession—the thing offered to him with no strings attached except to love the master and his work well enough to advance it in his absence. But advance it how far? That's what we want to know. We think this story is about doubling something. We think it's about outcomes or measurable results. It's not. Need I remind you that all of this—from the five talents to the one talent—was little to the master. He didn't need it—he could accomplish his plans with or without these servants. Nevertheless, he had invited them to share in the joy of the labor, as well as the joy of the relationship they would develop through the sharing. And his hope was to invite this man into that same relationship.

God doesn't need us in order to be God. But he invites us into his kingdom as players and participants as he expands the footprint of his kingdom in the hearts of others. This is a key theological point for the modern mind, which tends to think it is the spoke in the wheel. We live as if the kingdom of God rises and falls on our fruitfulness—and yes, God has allowed his work of redemption in this world to be represented, sometimes for better and sometimes for worse, by the attitudes and actions of his bride, who is waiting for him to return for the ultimate wedding.

But we shouldn't think he is limited to our actions or confined by our failures or successes. We are merely beloved servants who get to work in *his* fields; but he has a billion other fields—boundless power, strength, wisdom, insight, and the like—by which he will accomplish his ultimate goals in exactly the way he has planned to do since before the foundations of this world. And part of this plan is to invite us in to participate in his plan, for his kingdom, with his resources, as his servants. This is why he uses the prophet Isaiah to proclaim:

> "Remember this and stand firm,
> > recall it to mind, you transgressors,
> > remember the former things of old;
> for I am God, and there is no other;
> > I am God, and there is none like me,
> *declaring the end from the beginning*
> > *and from ancient times things not yet done,*
> saying, 'My counsel shall stand,
> > and *I will accomplish all my purpose.'"*
> > > > > *Isaiah 46:8–10, emphasis mine*

In other words, the master didn't need a financial return on the tiny investments he had entrusted to his servants. His goal was that they would follow in his footsteps—the works that reflect the culture of his kingdom—and thus share in the joy of this kingdom and of the relationship with him they would develop through it. He wasn't counting on a financial return to make ends meet. He was hopeful for a partnership based on relationship and effective for the sake of the world. Imagine not only the blessing of entering the joy of the master but also the return on investment that could have been realized if the one-talent guy had just done something! In ministry, this return equates to souls saved, lives changed, marriages healed, families restored, addicts set free, hungry people fed, and so much more. Instead, the resource was buried.

THE PROBLEM WITH FEAR

It was the faulty belief of the third servant that led him to take faulty action with his master's investment—and this exact sequence always occurs when there is faulty belief in our hearts about the heart of God. The servant did not believe the master was someone he could ever truly please, so he disregarded the greatest chance of his life to participate in the grandiose adventure of purposing himself toward his master's kingdom. He didn't realize what really pleased the master, which was his heart to join in the work of his kingdom.

An important note here: the servant didn't receive a harsh judgment simply because he had a good or bad heart, didn't catch the right breaks, or didn't come from the right family. The excuse making of Christianity that permeates much of church culture today is dangerous. It teaches us that God will be fine with his expectation of us, no matter what we do, as long as we mean well. After all, God "knows our hearts." One part of this is correct: he does indeed know our hearts. In fact, Scripture says that, actually, we cannot know our own hearts because they are "deceitful above all things, and desperately sick."[2] It's because he knows our hearts that he sent Jesus to transform them and bring us into alignment with his kingdom.

And so just trying harder and hoping for the best is not our best life now—not in the least. Remember, we are not spiritual paupers, no matter what our ministry or church situation may be. We are investors who work for a multi-universenaire (that is, he owns everything there is in the universe, as well as what's outside of it).

Stewardship done well—that which will someday receive a "well done"—involves using the treasures you've been given out of a genuine trust that the Master knew what he was doing when he entrusted them to you. While these may include your personal gifts, talents, abilities, charisma, and disposition, the treasure certainly entails so much more, namely, the gospel itself as shared and transmitted to the hearts of everyone we meet, which is the incalculable "power of God for salvation to everyone who believes,"[3] as well as "the riches of his glorious inheritance in the saints"[4]—in other words, in the people who make up Christ's body, his church.

The Master doesn't want a bunch of servants running around just staying busy in ministry, simply trying harder with no direction or purpose, doing church the best they can without any regard for the culture of the Master's kingdom. The treasures themselves— the gospel and God's people—are what we are supposed to invest all of our energy into with joyful trust and evident care because we believe rightly that they are also precious to the Master.

But not believing rightly led the third servant to an unnecessary place—to fear of the master.[5] As Paul and John both remind us, when we fear God's wrath and the day we will settle accounts with him as stewards, we fail to understand "the immeasurable riches of his grace in kindness toward us in Christ Jesus,"[6] as well as the very basics of the whole point of the gospel—to "come to know and to believe the love that God has for us," because "by *this* is love perfected with us, so that we may have confidence for the day of judgment, because as he is so also are we in this world. There is no fear in love, but perfect love casts out fear. For fear has to do with punishment, and whoever fears has not been perfected [achieved maturity] in love."[7]

Can you sense the tone of assurance and stability in these

passages? They invite us to a proper viewpoint of the Master that takes away our fear of his present and future judgment, thus freeing us to be about the work of his kingdom as trusted stewards rather than fearful servants who always worry that the Master's real desire is to hurt us. Fear of God's wrath is the very thing Jesus came to dismiss by taking all of that wrath on himself: "For God has not destined us for wrath, but to obtain salvation through our Lord Jesus Christ, who died for us so that whether we are awake or asleep we might live with him."[8] Again, the goal of the Master for his servants has always been that we might *live with him*. That is the reward. That is the goal.

But if we don't trust the Master's heart toward us, we can't live as good stewards because we are bypassing the basic foundational premise of the whole relationship—the goodness and generosity of the Master. The result wasn't good for the one-talent servant, but make no mistake, it wasn't about the results he failed to produce but rather about his faulty belief in the nature of the master. He wasn't given a "well done, good and faithful servant" but was instead called lazy, slothful, and wicked. He revealed his wickedness not just by his actions but more so by the belief (or lack thereof) that birthed his actions. His lack of work was merely a reflection of his lack of trust in and love for his master.

SEEKING DOUBLE VERSUS SEEKING FAITHFUL

As we've explored in depth in previous chapters, the modern mind tends to want to quantify—to ascribe the greatest worth to whatever has highest value in terms of raw data or numbers. But this is not the way of the Father. He measures worth by more than raw numbers, and our daily invitation as believers and leaders is to align ourselves with his kingdom culture and what he evaluates as worthy.

This seems counterintuitive to this story in particular because it appears that the master is upset with the third servant because he hasn't produced as much return on investment as the other two servants. This is simply not the case, which is evidenced by the fact that the master told the servant, "Then you ought to have invested my money with the bankers, and at my coming I should have received what was my own with interest."[9]

Though I can't speak with certainty, I believe that if the servant had done this bare minimum of investing the money with bankers for a return of simple interest, this story would have ended a different way. Why? Because the heart of the master was not to compare him to the other servants. He did not say to the third servant, "You should have done what the other two servants did." No, it is *our* hearts that say this to the third servant because we are locked into a culture of comparison in ways we don't even realize. A more accurate viewpoint of the master in this story is that he was longing to say, "Well done!" to every servant—including this one—because he loved them all the same, which is why he entrusted to them the very work of his kingdom.

The master wasn't mad because the servant hadn't produced the same return of ten talents and four talents. We are the ones who get stuck in the rut of comparison and calculations here, teaching that the master expected a double return on his investment—which for the third servant would have been a two-talent return. We spend our lives thinking we have to "double it," whatever *it* may be. But the heart of the master here is profoundly gracious, even in his correction. He basically tells the servant that if he had just done *something* with what he had been given, it would have revealed that his heart understood and desired to emulate the heart of his master. He would have said, "Well done!"

to the third servant as well. But there was nothing for him to evaluate, which itself was an evaluation of the way the servant viewed the master.

Good stewardship begins with good belief about a good Master. Everything flows from there, and nothing eternally good can flow unless it begins there, even if good earthly results are present. It is not our job to necessarily double everything that comes into our metaphorical hands in this life, though I hope God enables you to do so in yours.

God's church should grow, because healthy things grow. Don't let that feel like a contradiction of what I've said above. Jesus came to seek and save those who are lost and to add them to his kingdom. But even more than fruitfulness, God desires faithfulness. I am concerned that some of us have sacrificed faithfulness on the idolatrous altar of fruitfulness. We think God is impressed with how fruitful we are, and we'll do all we can to see fruitfulness come to bear.

While God wants his kingdom to grow and has resourced us according to his view of our capacity to be fruitful within his kingdom, God rewards faithfulness. Pastor, leader, minister, Christian worker, board member, denominational leader, please know that God will bring fruitfulness; you just bring faithfulness. Don't ever be caught holding God's original investment.

In terms of countable metrics of things like attendance, income, influence, abilities, and the like, I believe God isn't looking for every tree to bear the same number of pieces of fruit. Again, he knows what every tree—every servant—is capable of, and he is calling us to be faithful to those capabilities.

And this success is not defined by how many pieces of fruit are produced; rather, it is defined by faithfulness to produce what each tree is divinely capable of producing. Faithfulness, not fruitfulness, is the crux of the matter in this particular parable.

After all, the master did not give higher praise to the five-talent servant than he did the two-talent servant because both had done the same amount of work. Both had been faithful with what had been graciously entrusted to them.

When we trust the heart of the Master and believe he gives opportunity based on what he knows we are capable of—and that even the minimum of what he entrusts to the "least" of us is still nothing less than millions—we can stop trying to match the fruit of every other church, leader, or pastor around us. If we recast this parable as a church growth parable (though it is certainly much more than that and applies to every believer in every situation), it is obvious that each servant didn't see their church grow to the same size. But the fact remained that they each were granted something of great worth that wasn't their own, and two out of the three understood the joy of this entitlement. The third found it bothersome because he didn't trust the master.

Please don't forget that the leader who was entrusted with eighty-five people in his church will walk into heaven next to the guy who was entrusted with fifty thousand people—and both will have nothing in their hands, because those people weren't theirs in the first place. The same rings true for any believer in any personal or professional endeavor, because the principles of "church" are the same as the principles of life; that is, they are merely the principles of God. The question won't be "how many?" It will be "how faithful?" And that has been a central ethic for how I try to lead at LifePoint Church—faithfully free, with an open hand on what is not mine to begin with.

If you happen to be a one-talent servant and your situation, ability, or circumstance doesn't seem to produce huge bushels of fruit in terms of people in your church, then remember the lesson taught in this parable. While you may not be as low on talents as you think, the principles are unchanging. Do you joyfully trust that the Master knew what he was doing when he began a good work in you? If so, this *trust in him* will lead you to faithfulness in his *entrustment to you*. Incidentally, I don't like the minimizing of a one-talent perspective. It's still twenty years of value. It's still about real people who really matter to our real God. I'm deeply grateful for a small start—and I don't know when the promotion actually takes place. I'm going to keep working this one talent I was given until my Master Jesus comes to get it.

If the master in the story said that the servant should have invested in a bank for interest, which would be anywhere from a 1 to 3 percent return in today's banking environment, then perhaps we should be okay with a 1 percent growth in our churches—*if,* that is, we are placing our energies into constantly trusting the heart of the Master. (And by growth, I don't mean just numerical growth, but also disciple making, community impact, widespread freedom from life-controlling issues and social oppression, and the like.) This will also lead us into being enthusiastically faithful to shepherd God's people into the culture of his kingdom. When you are faithful, God may decide to also make you more fruitful. I am still shocked that he continues to entrust more people into our field—and there may be days ahead when he decides to decrease that number. But no matter what, we know that these people are not ours.

And your people aren't yours either, so just be faithful to the gospel—to being and making disciples according to the culture of God's kingdom. After all, it's not our job to grow his church; it's our job to continually grow more faithful as devoted followers of Christ.

This process of faithfully helping people grow in their relationship with God is the real work of the kingdom, and it is big work, no matter how small our churches may be. Yes, I do believe that healthy things tend to grow, but the bottom line is that not every leader is the same and not every positive outcome is explosive numerical growth. I may not be a five-talent guy just because LifePoint Church has grown fast and big. I believe myself to be more of a one-talent guy, and this is what the minimal interest gains of trying to be faithful looks like in a town like Clarksville. Similarly, you may be a five-talent person in a town of two thousand people, reaching someone with your faithfulness that no one else bothers to notice, and God may consider yours a doubling of his investment. Because he's not just looking at numbers; he's evaluating on a kingdom level.

For others, this means that just because your church is big, you shouldn't necessarily assume your talents have been doubled. Healthy things grow, but so do unhealthy or less desirable things like weeds, nose hairs, and cancerous tumors. Everything in your hands as a leader will be turned in to the Master, so the real question is not how much you've grown the church (which, if we believe Scripture, is not something *we* can do at all) but how faithful you've been in helping people see and find the path to becoming real disciples. How faithful have you been in promoting the kingdom of God in the lives of the people you are called to pastor? Work the dirt of their hearts, welcome the missing, make room for those who need a seat, disciple people far from God, and more. That is our objective—to be found faithful there. Let God grow the thing, but let us tend the thing faithfully.

Chris Hodges—my pastor and one of my mentors—laid out this path of discipleship in his book *Four Cups*. Pastor Chris demonstrates how God made four distinct promises in Exodus 6:6–7: "I'm going to save you. I'm going to deliver you. I'm going to redeem you. You're going to be my people, and I'll be your God."[10] This is a process followed in all of Scripture for the way God works in the lives of people: they find salvation through his grace; they are delivered from whatever enslaves and hinders them in this life; they find redemptive purpose; and they make a difference in the lives of people because they themselves are God's people.

Wherever you are, steward yourself and your leadership to focus everything on these processes, because when you do, you will appropriately and faithfully manage the church God has given you. You can't wish away the place where you are. You can't spend your time and energies thinking, *If we can just break the five hundred person barrier, we can really focus on the deeper things.* This attitude doesn't trust the master's discerned entrustment. Be faithful at the two hundred person mark, and as the Lord desires, he may bring you to the five hundred mark. But he may not. Remember that it all gets turned back in at the end, and we all receive the same reward—living in his joy with him for eternity, which is infinitely more fulfilling than watching our church attendance double in size.

What does it look like to be faithful with the people God has given you? What does it mean to enjoy the taupe building, along with the challenges of where you presently find yourself? It means you keep moving your people toward knowing God and the purposes revealed in Scripture to find freedom, discover purpose, make a difference, and the like.

It also means that sometimes we'll be serving next to people who don't particularly match our own leadership profiles, but the Lord put us together in the same church. For example, a lot of churches these days have a fresh style and approach, blue lights and smoke, great music, and trendy-dressed leadership. But our church is filled with soldiers, men, new believers, and a lot of folks who are brand-new to Christ—and even newer to trendy Christianity. I can't refuse to acknowledge the kind of people I have because some research somewhere shows that another style is better for church growth. I must be faithful to make deeper disciples of the actual disciples who are with me. Our context speaks to the way the kingdom of God genuinely looks and sounds. We don't copy the talents of others who are growing churches. We invest in *this* context and let God bring growth to *this* expression.

Some of our leaders are gray-haired. Some of our leaders aren't very polished. Some of the folks who lead are still shedding their own baggage. They may not fit the profile of what most explosively growing churches are looking for, but they are huge talents that God has given us. We've been blessed by their faithfulness, which God uses to increase our fruitfulness.

I can't be faithful with what God has given somebody else, but that seems to be the current trend in the church world. How could I ever be faithful with the vision that God gave Pastor Chris Hodges or Bishop T. D. Jakes? While I can learn from them—and I do—I don't need to spend my time trying to imitate and reproduce the culture of the churches they lead in their own cities. I need to be faithful to those God has put in our path. If God has given you a bunch of farmers, soldiers, or retired New York bankers, be faithful to steward well their growth through the steps of discipleship.

The reason the master found two of his three servants to be faithful was that they did something with what he had entrusted to them. Faithfulness had nothing to do with their fruitfulness. Faithfulness was just what they did. But be careful, many of us have embraced the idolatry of fruitfulness instead of a commitment to faithfulness. We celebrate the story because of the wrong things, but the good master desired to celebrate with every one of his servants, regardless of the technicality of their increases.

Our Master desires the same thing for us.

GO LIVE YOUR
OWN PARABLE

Here we are at the end of our time together, but I pray that it is truly another beginning for you as you reflect not just on these three parables but also on the culture of Christ's kingdom revealed in all of his parables and teachings. There's so much there to ground you in the right mindset of the gospel.

Imagine what church would be like if everything that matters to Christ mattered just as much to us. Actually, we don't have to imagine. Our ministries, programs, and sermons should not be designed to show everyone how much Greek we may pretend to know. Everything we do is about calling lost people to repentance and saved people to devotion within the "feel" of Christ's culture—one of honesty, generosity, invitation, graciousness, and power.

These goals will be met not in programming but in what Jesus will do in someone's heart after the preparation that occurs through honest engagement, humility, true communities of authenticity, and faithfulness to the biblical principles of making fully devoted disciples. This can only be done in real community with real people who also desire to steward well the party, the field, and the talents God has entrusted to each of us.

The goal of the Christian life and of leading and pastoring people is *not* to grow a big church, but rather to serve others and be faithful to share and express the culture of the kingdom of God, the culture of the Father, the culture of our Master.

ACKNOWLEDGMENTS

Thank you, John Driver, for helping craft my voice from preacher to author! You're such an amazing friend and brother.

Thank you, Asbury Theological Seminary, for believing in this project and for your support.

Thank you, Pastor Chris Hodges, for calling out some things you saw in me, which helped me write this for others.

Thank you, Pastor Rod Loy, for your generosity toward me, and for your patience and consistent encouragement.

Thank you, Dr. Doug Oss, for teaching me to treat Scripture with such priority and to expose the deeper stuff.

Thank you to the amazing staff of LifePoint Church. Your thoughts and prayers are in this book. Long talks, whiteboard sessions, and office chats have helped this book come alive. You truly are an amazing team!

NOTES

Chapter 1: Jesus Said What?

1. No one actually "does" church like Jesus did church. We have no record that he led weekly worship songs or gathered a traditional offering. His ministry was nomadic, carried out on the road, traveling from town to town. And ultimately it ended in crucifixion.
2. This is not meant to insinuate that all Catholic churches or experiences are this way—not in the least. But Blane's was.
3. The term *prophetic* means a lot of different things to a lot of different people, but later in the book, I'll clarify what I mean by it. I would wager that I mean it in a different way from the way you're probably thinking of it. Stay tuned.
4. See John 13:35.
5. I will share the process of how we studied these parables, and what they revealed, later in the book. It was one of the most powerful revelations we've ever experienced.
6. Here I'm borrowing from the subtitle to Todd Wagner's book *Come and See: Everything You Ever Wanted in the One Place You Would Never Look* (Colorado Springs: Cook, 2017).
7. I have repeated this exercise multiple times with focus groups, church staffs I have coached, small groups, and pastoral roundtables. The results are consistent in all groups.
8. Of course I'm referring to the 1993 movie *Tombstone*, starring Kurt Russell and Val Kilmer.

Chapter 2: Lost Things Matter

1. Luke 15:1–2.
2. I encourage you to read the actual biblical text as found in Luke 15:11–31.
3. Most dictionaries use this definition as well.
4. Drought led to famines in the time of Abraham (Genesis 12:10), Isaac (Genesis 26:1), Joseph (Genesis 41:27), and the judges (Ruth 1:1). Famine also laid waste to the Israelites in the days of David (2 Samuel 21:1), Elijah (1 Kings 18:2), Elisha (2 Kings 4:38), Haggai (Haggai 1:11), and Nehemiah (Nehemiah 5:3). And famine continued during the time of the prophets as well.

Chapter 3: The Father's Economy

1. For one of the most transformative reflections on the true meaning of the Beatitudes, I point you to chapter 4 of Dallas Willard's classic work *The Divine Conspiracy* (San Francisco: HarperSanFrancisco, 1998), 97–127.
2. This is a major point made by Dallas Willard (see *The Divine Conspiracy*, chapter 4; see also 132–34).
3. Craig S. Keener, *The IVP Bible Background Commentary: New Testament* (Downers Grove, IL: InterVarsity, 1993), 230.
4. I urge you to read Tim Keller's *The Prodigal God: Recovering the Heart of the Christian Faith* (New York: Dutton, 2008). This whole concept is wonderfully developed there, and it further shows the nature of God as the truly prodigal one who continues to lavish his love and blessings on us.

Chapter 4: Throw a Party

1. Matthew 12:34.
2. 1 Peter 4:8.
3. James 4:6.
4. See Romans 2:4.
5. Romans 5:8, emphasis mine.
6. 1 Corinthians 14:32.

Chapter 5: Seeds, Soil, and Such

1. "Outreach Magazine Celebrates America's Fastest-Growing Churches," *Outreach*, October 16, 2018, https://outreachmag azine.com/features/megachurch/36058-outreach-magazine -celebrates-americas-fastest-growing-churches.html.
2. See 1 Corinthians 3:4–9.
3. Matthew 13:10.
4. Navel-gazing is slang for excessive introspection, self-absorption, or concentration on a single issue. It's an overinfatuation with your belly button . . . or some random part of yourself. Thank you, Dr. Doug Oss, for giving me such a fun term to use.
5. Hebrews 4:12.
6. Romans 1:16.
7. See 1 Corinthians 1:24.
8. 1 Corinthians 1:18 NASB.

Chapter 6: Turning Over the Soil

1. See Luke 9:46–48.
2. See Luke 9:51–56.
3. See John 18:15–27.
4. See Mark 14:47.
5. See John 20:26–29.
6. See John 12:6; Matthew 26:14–16.
7. Right after Jesus performed one of the most famous miracles, feeding five thousand people with a little boy's lunch, he offended the masses by telling them to eat his flesh and drink his blood. John 6:66 reveals that many of them stopped following Jesus after that, choosing to take him literally instead of continuing to follow him as a lifestyle, even when the bread and fish ran out.
8. See John 13:35.
9. See Acts 20:7–12.
10. Philippians 1:21.

Chapter 7: Seeds among Stones and Thorns

1. Matthew 13:20–21 NASB.
2. See Matthew 7:26–27.
3. Jeremiah 6:16.
4. The American pastor and evangelist Charles Finney (1792–1875) was known as a primary voice of leadership in the second Great Awakening and is thought by some to be the inventor of the altar call.
5. Ephesians 4:4, 6.
6. Quoted in Calvin Miller, ed., *The Book of Jesus: A Treasury of the Greatest Stories and Writings about Christ* (New York: Simon & Schuster, 1996), 206.
7. Philippians 2:13.
8. See Hebrews 4:12.
9. See Matthew 16:18.

Chapter 8: It's All His

1. U.S. Census Bureau, "Real Median Household Income in the United States," Federal Reserve Bank of St. Louis: Economic Research, September 10, 2019, https://fred.stlouisfed.org/series/MEHOINUSA672N.
2. These figures align with estimates found in many study Bibles with regard to the amounts disbursed, but there are multiple opinions among scholars on the exact amounts. My point, as you will see, is not to overemphasize the ancient to modern exchange rate or debate the quantifiable possibilities, but rather to make it clear that what was given to each servant was a substantial, not a stingy, amount.
3. Ephesians 3:8.
4. Ephesians 1:18.
5. Colossians 2:9–10 NASB, emphasis mine.
6. 2 Peter 1:3, emphasis mine.
7. Matthew 25:23, emphasis mine.

Chapter 9: What's Yours Is Not Mine

1. Matthew 25:15, emphasis mine.
2. The following details are found in 2 Timothy 4:9–22.
3. 2 Timothy 4:10.
4. 2 Timothy 4:16.

Chapter 10: Don't Just Grow . . . Grow Faithful

1. See Hebrews 4:12.
2. Jeremiah 17:9.
3. Romans 1:16.
4. Ephesians 1:18.
5. See Matthew 25:25.
6. Ephesians 2:7.
7. 1 John 4:16–18, emphasis mine.
8. 1 Thessalonians 5:9–10.
9. Matthew 25:27.
10. See Chris Hodges, *Four Cups: God's Timeless Promises for a Life of Fulfillment* (Wheaton, IL: Tyndale, 2014), 6.